# Be Thou My Vision
*MEDITATIONS ON THE PRIESTHOOD*

Bishop David L. Ricken, DD, JCL
with Father Clifford Stevens

THE INSTITUTE FOR PRIESTLY FORMATION
IPF PUBLICATIONS

THE INSTITUTE FOR PRIESTLY FORMATION
IPF PUBLICATIONS
2500 California Plaza
Omaha, Nebraska 68178
www.IPFpublications.com

Printed in the United States of America
ISBN-13: 978-0-9800455-7-4
ISBN-10: 0-9800455-7-6

Cover design by Timothy D. Boatright
Marketing Associates, U.S.A.
Tampa, Florida

## THE INSTITUTE FOR PRIESTLY FORMATION
### Mission Statement

The Institute for Priestly Formation was founded to assist bishops in the spiritual formation of diocesan seminarians and priests in the Roman Catholic Church. The Institute responds to the need to foster spiritual formation as the integrating and governing principle of all aspects of priestly formation. Inspired by the biblical-evangelical spirituality of Ignatius Loyola, this spiritual formation has as its goal the cultivation of a deep interior communion with Christ; from such communion the priest shares in Christ's own pastoral charity. In carrying out its mission, the Institute directly serves diocesan seminarians and priests as well as those who are responsible for diocesan priestly formation.

THE INSTITUTE FOR PRIESTLY FORMATION
Creighton University
2500 California Plaza
Omaha, Nebraska 68178
www.creighton.edu/ipf
ipf@creighton.edu

# Be Thou My Vision

Translated by Eleanor Hull

*Be thou my vision, O Lord of my heart,*
*Naught is all else to me, save that Thou art.*
*Thou my best thought by day and by night,*
*Waking or sleeping, Thy presence my light.*

*Be thou my wisdom, Thou my true word;*
*I ever with Thee, Thou with me, Lord.*
*Thou my great father, I Thy dear son;*
*Thou in me dwelling, I with Thee one.*

*Be Thou my battle-shield, sword for the fight,*
*Be Thou my dignity, Thou my delight.*
*Thou my soul's shelter, Thou my high tower;*
*Raise Thou me heavenward, power of my power.*

*Riches I heed not, nor man's empty praise,*
*Thou mine inheritance now and always.*
*Thou, and Thou only, first in my heart,*
*High king of heaven, my treasure Thou art.*

*King of the seven heavens, grant me for dole,*
*Thy love in my heart, Thy light in my soul.*
*Thy light from my soul, Thy love from my heart,*
*King of the seven heavens, may they never depart,*

*With the high king of heaven, after victory won,*
*May I reach heaven's joys, O bright heaven's sun!*
*Heart of my own heart, whatever befall,*
*Still be my vision, O Ruler of all.*

# Dedication

To the priests who have inspired, encouraged, and had a formative effect on my priesthood throughout the years:

Father Joseph Bahr
Monsignor Norbert Temaat
Father Clifford Stevens
Most Reverend Arthur N. Tafoya
Monsignor Charles Elmer

# Table of Contents

# The Horizons of Priesthood

*"I remind you to stir into flame the gift of God that you have through the imposition of my hands. For God did not give us a spirit of cowardice but rather of power and love and self-control. So do not be ashamed of your testimony to our Lord."*

2 Tim. 1:6-8

In April 1947, Father Walter Farrell, the luminous Dominican priest who died at the young age of forty-nine, wrote an article for *The Thomist* entitled "Twentieth Century Apostle." In it, he pre-dated the priestly vision of Vatican Council II and some of the stirring words of Pope John Paul II to the priests of the world. Father Farrell tried to show the unlimited possibilities of a dedicated and vibrant priesthood and the critical role of the priest in scattering the darkness and hopelessness of the modern world. He compared the work of the priest of today with the work of the original band of Apostles, who set out to conquer the world for Christ in such an astonishing and amazing way:

> The strategy of that original band of Apostles was never purely defensive because it was never purely human; it was definitely offensive. It was not negative but positive. They were not fighting off something nearly so much as they were bringing something home: happiness to unhappy men, joy to sad pagans, strength and hope to beaten fighters, relief to men so miserable they had forgotten there was anything

but misery. Their program was not so much one of reform as relief, not so much corrective as informing and inspiring.[1]

The theme of this book arose out of Father Farrell's writing: What is the root reality of priestly and apostolic effectiveness? What is the one indispensable quality that a priest must possess if he is to be more than a clerical functionary?

> The most powerful expression of what has laid hold of the mind and heart of a man is not what he writes or says, but what he does and is ... the supreme apostolic weapon of the original Apostles was their very lives and actions. Short of the grace of God, it was their life exposition of the message of Christ that made the modern world Christian.... Men read and doubted, they heard and argued, but when they *saw*, they fell on their knees. It is not literature, it is not oratory, but sanctity that can bring happiness to men.[2]

The Catholic priesthood is the divinely established instrument for the evangelization of the world. Keeping alive the vision of the Gospels and the Mystery of the Incarnation, source of the Gospels, priesthood is a critical element in the fruitfulness of the human race and the spiritual health of individuals. Its unique power and transforming influence are evident in the lives of peoples and nations and in the creation of remarkable cultural achievements that have endured through the ages. Wherever the Catholic priesthood has flourished, human life has been enriched immeasurably;

where it has waned, whole nations and peoples have been left desolate and impoverished. Since the priest is the primary instrument for carrying out the pastoral mission of the Church in every age and century, in every time and place, the health and effectiveness of that pastoral mission is dependent upon the quality of priesthood and the priest's vision of priestly identity.

Three pillars of Christian spirituality were formulated long ago by masters of the spiritual life: (1) the mystic order of grace, (2) the sapiential order of truth, and (3) the human order of virtue. I wish to write about the third pillar with regard to the priesthood. Virtue gives the priesthood an epic quality that is seen in the lives of great priests, especially those who have *Saint* before their names.

When virtues are a living and vital wellspring of a priestly personality, they assist us in reaching for the unreachable, transforming us into creative geniuses in furthering the work of Jesus Christ. It is possible to take our work too seriously and ourselves not seriously enough. We are not just laborers for hire. As workers in the vineyard of the Lord, we are extensions of Jesus Christ to the world and to the people we serve. Attention to real and important details of daily responsibilities may cause us to suffer a loss of vision, blurring the fullness of our mission in Jesus Christ. Our parish, position, or assignment can easily fill the horizon, and we can lose sight of our priestly character, forgetting that we are not laborers for hire or in pursuit of a professional career but sharers in the very priesthood of Christ.

Brushing shoulders with professional men and women every day, in Medicine, Law, Business, Science, the

11

Arts, Government, and Politics, we can easily assume the career instincts of the professional man—instincts that are right and proper for those who serve the City of Man. But we serve the City of God on a more explicit level than any others in society, and our labors reach beyond the horizons of this world—and touch Eternity. We are Christ's men, and the moment we forget that, we can become like the Monsignor in the book *True Confessions,* who felt that he could further the work of the Church by associating with the rich and powerful—and who destroyed himself by some rather unsavory associations. Or the priest in J. F. Powers's *Morte d'Urban,* a classical study in spiritual mediocrity, about a priest who becomes something of a wheeler-dealer for his religious order and forgets what his priesthood is really all about. Every priest encounters these types of temptations, and we must recognize when we are in danger of taking the first step in the wrong direction.

A most important reason for prayerfully recalling the true nature of the priesthood is to combat both *institutional fatigue* and *emotional burnout.* The first comes from spreading ourselves too thin in the demands of our priestly work, and the second is the result of letting our spiritual roots run dry. The concept of institutional fatigue is captured in a popular verse that can be applied to any kind of overwork. It describes what happens when a person spreads himself too thin:

> If you keep your nose to the grindstone rough,
> And keep it down there long enough,
> Soon there will be no such thing
> As the brooks that babble or the birds that sing.

Three things alone will your life compose:
The stone, the hurt ... and your darned old nose.

The concept of burnout is expressed in another verse that tells the story very well:

There was an old monk from Siberia,
Whose life became wearier and wearier.
One day with a shout, He said, "I've got to get out!"
And ran off with the Mother Superior![3]

The nature of our priesthood can be threatened in a three-fold way:

1. In the present: routine and boredom, and being overwhelmed by the needs, labors, and necessities of the moment and the weariness and fatigue that follow these.

2. In the past: forgetfulness, being unmindful of God's presence in our life, the great realities of faith saying nothing to us, insensitivity or even coolness toward God, the failure to cultivate any sense of His providence or His goodness to us—a form of spiritual blindness.

3. In the future: lack of enthusiasm for the work of the priesthood, the eclipse of the eternal, complete lack of vision, a life drained of hope, no real dependence on the providence of God, grim prospects for the immediate future, cynicism, and a jaded view of our own priestly work.

We should not think these dangers are uncommon. They are all around us. They can become the *culture*, the climate, the very atmosphere in which we live and breathe. We live in an almost totally pagan and secular world, and we simply cannot pretend that we do not inhale its fetid air. To protect ourselves from this atmosphere, we need to breathe a different air, one that is saturated with sacramental consciousness and the Gifts of the Holy Spirit.

All of us are born with a unique temperament and personality. I rejoice in the variety of priests that I find in my own diocese: Each one is a gem, carefully polished by a unique education and experience that makes for delightful conversations and sharing as I make my way around the diocese. But there is one quality for which I look and for which I am deeply grateful when I find it: a man who builds up the Church spiritually by his love for Christ's Bride.

We forget that religion cannot be forced; we can only invite others into the love that has beguiled us. This acceptance of God's love for us will transform us and attract others by that very transformation. We cannot let our temperament interfere with drawing people to God; we must allow God to change us. Whether we recognize it or not, we are instruments.

Yes, people can get under our skin; they can irritate and try our patience; they can be unreasonable, sometimes vicious and malicious, and can drive us to distraction—if we let them. But one act of rudeness, one moment of impatience, one sharp or unkind word can undo years of dedication, hard work, and devotion. Some priests learn that lesson through bitter experience. Some never learn it at all, and I have never heard it discussed at priestly gatherings or in books on pastoral theology.

The problems and difficulties we face are very seldom of our own making. Such problems are part of the *very nature* of priestly work and are not always due to our own incompetence, a failure in our character, or a flaw in our personality. One needs only to look at the history of the priesthood or the life of any saint or priest who accomplished or tried to accomplish *anything* for God to see that obstacles, problems, and difficulties *are part of the very nature of the work* and not a sign of personal failure or God's disapproval. The only real problem we have is *discouragement*, and *there is never a reason for discouragement.*

We tend to blame ourselves for what seem to be our failures or to see them as a testing ground created by God. Some obstacles come from the *very nature of priestly work*; they cannot be avoided, and they are not due to our own stupidity, impracticality, or lack of judgment. Once we realize this, we can put our efforts where they really belong and not use them as ammunition for self-recrimination or cause for discouragement. The danger, then, is that we will begin to see ourselves as unequal to the tasks we have to face. This is really the most powerful tool in the devil's arsenal, and many priests have withered under this sense of inadequacy. Trust God and Him alone. God leads us in the way *He* wants us to go, not necessarily in the way *we* prefer to go. In the hectic business of being a priest today, we can easily lose sight of a personal providence, that we are the objects of God's conscious and constant attention. He is aware of us—every step we take, every crisis we face, every task and work to which we put our hand. We are never out of His sight or His tender, watchful care.

The apparent silence of God is one of the most agonizing problems in the spiritual life of a priest. There is a medieval, Latin poem called *Carmen Paschale*. The author, an Irish poet named Caelius Sedulius, visualizes Jesus quieting the tempest, a testament to the poet's own faith in the power of Christ extended into his own century. Sedulius saw the Gospels as a living witness to God's mastery of the universe and His action upon human history, rather than a merely historical account of God's action in the past:

> The Lord arising bade the winds be still.
> The swelling waves subsided at His word—
> Not even ocean when its deeps are stirred
> With fellest rage resists ...
> The happy sea to Christ in homage brings
> Its lofty billows down; the tempest springs
> Its joy away on softly wafting wings.[4]

Some people seem to have lost hope in the conviction that God is the Lord of human history and that He shapes history to His own intentions. Historical tempests are no more fierce than the tempests of nature that the living Lord faced in the moments of His historical existence, and He is quite as capable of stepping into the picture and calming the tempest now as then. If the Incarnation tells us anything, it is that we are not alone in the universe and that God is still its master. However fierce the tempest, He still commands the wind and the waves.

Today, the Catholic priesthood is lashed by such a tempest—not for the first time in history but certainly for the first time within our memory. Whether it be the newspaper headlines and the television news screaming the scandal of priests betraying their vocation, the scandal of dioceses on the brink of bankruptcy, or the tempest that rages between various factions in the Church, the effect is the same: demoralization and discouragement among priests. The tempest may grow stronger as the shortage of priests becomes critical, and the workload of the individual priest will stretch his endurance to the limit. Amidst the storm, God can still quiet the winds and the waves, and He will do so in His time. We must hold fast to Him in our small boat, however fierce the winds and however frightening the waves.

We do not enter into the priesthood as a man enters the Army or Navy, or as someone becomes a doctor or a lawyer, or even as a president takes office. We are chosen specifically and personally by Jesus Christ for a definite task, in a definite part of the world-wide Church, at a definite time and place in history. Whatever that task may be and wherever our place of labor is, He is with us and beside us every step of the way. We are living extensions of Jesus Christ, and once we lose sight of this truth, we lose the most powerful tool in our spiritual arsenal: a living sense of that bond we have with Jesus Christ, with the God Who created us and led into the priesthood. As Father Walter Farrell wrote: "Happiness can shrink from too much contact with despair, secrets can be smothered by scorn, and fires can die down, if fuel is not fed them, even Divine fires if they burn in the hearts of men." The fuel is the bond we have with the Divine, the source of our vocation and our strength, our hope, and our optimism. Again, Father Walter Farrell:

> The Apostles might have looked out over their world and wondered how to prevent

the obliteration of the infant Church by the crushing weight of paganism, as a modern priest might wonder how to avert the submergence of the Church today under the growing waves of un-Christian thought and practice. In actual fact, this was not the problem of the Apostles. Their problem was how to convert a world, not avert then convert. It could not be otherwise, for the first is a purely human point of view, edging fearfully towards despair under the weight of the overwhelming probabilities of defeat; the second is beyond the reach of man, unless he stands on the shoulders of God, a prospect alive with hope, with challenge, and vibrant with courage.[5]

What kind of optimism can we have in times like these, when the horizons are so dark and the Church seems to be going through a great crisis? Optimism! We will be lucky if we simply survive, if we come through every day without a new scandal or crisis beating down our spirits. How can anyone have optimism at a time like this?

What kind of faith is it, though, that operates only in sunshine? What kind of faith lives only in the bright light of day, only when things are going well, only when we see success, triumph, and victory everywhere? Were we not told by the Lord Himself that there would be dark days, that some of us would be brought before tribunals and persecutors, that there would be times when everything would be black and bleak?

The poem by G.K. Chesterton, called "The Ballad of the White Horse," is about England in the Dark Ages, in the days of King Alfred the Great. Hordes of pagan Vikings were sweeping down through England, ravaging everything, with violence and murder on every side, and churches, monasteries, even cities, left desolate and in ruins. The only hope was the King, Alfred, who gathered an army to fight the Vikings. In the poem, King Alfred stood in a chapel on a small island, wondering how to face the crisis, when Our Lady appeared to him, suspended just above a field of wheat. Falling on his knees and looking up at her, he asked: "Why are you coming to me? I am not worried about Heaven; I am worried about earth, about England, about the battle I am going to fight. Am I going to win?"

Our Lady gives him a very strange answer, and her words are not encouraging. She speaks lines that are famous in English literature, chiding him for his lack of faith:

> I tell you naught for your comfort,
> Yea, not for your desire.
> Save that the sky grows darker yet,
> And the sea rises higher.

> "Friend," she essentially says to him. "things
> are going to get worse."
> You and all the kind of Christ
> Are ignorant—and brave,
> And you have wars you hardly win,
> And souls you hardly save.

And then comes the punch line:

> The men of the East may study the stars
> To times and seasons mark,
> But those who are signed with the Cross of Christ
> Go gaily *in the dark*.[6]

Faith must sometimes walk in darkness, and we go gaily in the dark because we *know* the kind of God in whom we believe. He has promised to bring light out of darkness, victory out of defeat, strength out of weakness, and the help of the heavenly armies to those who serve Him.

If we are fearful and lack courage, and if we have faltered in our faith and stumbled in our trust, we must remember one thing: whenever we need courage, *there is One who will give it infallibly* if we ask for it. Do we actually believe that the millions of martyrs who died for the faith were courageous by nature—that they naturally held life in so little account? They all had courage because courage was necessary, and they had trust because trust was given to them. If we pray, what we need will certainly be given to us. We may have to go gaily in the dark, but strength and courage and trust will be given to us. If we do not truly believe *that*, then we should never have put on the collar that we are wearing.

We are only branches of the vine, and we should never forget that. Just as the vine sends its life-giving power through the shoots, so the True Vine, Jesus Christ, sends His power and strength through us, the branches of His Vine. We are not alone and have never been alone, and the work we are doing is not our own. How can we ever think that He could fail us in our time of need?

"Stir into flame the gift of God" (2 Tim. 1:6). Priest of Christ remember your dignity and your call. Christ is with you; He is unfailing in His promise toward you as priest. "I am with you always, until the end of the age" (Mt. 28:20).

# Notes

1     Walter Farrell, O.P., "Twentieth Century Apostle," *The Thomist* (April 1947). Reprinted in *Schema XIII: The Priest in the Modern World* I, no. 3 (March 1970): 4.

2     Ibid., 5.

3     Author unknown.

4     Caelius Sedulius, "Carmen Paschale" in *1,000 Years of Irish Poetry*, ed. Kathleen Hoagland, (Old Greenwich: Devin-Adair Publishing Co., 1947).

5     Farrell, 5.

6     G.K. Chesterton, "The Ballad of the White Horse," in *The Collected Poems of G.K. Chesterton*, (London: Methuen & Co. LTD, 1958).

# Works Cited

G.K. Chesterton, "The Ballad of the White Horse," in *The Collected Poems of G.K. Chesterton* (London: Methuen & Co. LTD, 1958).

John Gregory Dunne, *True Confessions* (Cambridge: De Capo Press, 2005).

Walter Farrell, O.P., "Twentieth Century Apostle," *The Thomist* (April 1947). Reprinted in *Schema XIII: The Priest in the Modern World* I, no. 3 (March 1970).

David L. Johns, *Mysticism and Ethics in Friedrich von Hügel* (Lewiston: Edwin Mellon, 2004).

Pope John Paul II, *Novo Millenio Ineunte*, 2001.

J.F. Powers, *Morte d'Urban* (New York: NYRB Classics, 2000).

Caelius Seduluis, "Carmen Paschale" in *1,000 Years of Irish Poetry*, ed. Ann Hoagland (Old Greenwich: Devin-Adair Publishing Co., 1947).

# Toward a Diocesan Priestly Spirituality

The challenge of ongoing formation in priestly spirituality is not a topic of spontaneous conversation at most priestly gatherings. Fifty years ago, every rectory had at least a dozen books on priestly spirituality, from classics like *The Spiritual Exercises of St. Ignatius* and *The Imitation of Christ* by Thomas à Kempis to *The Soul of the Apostolate* by the Cistercian Dom Chautard and *Christ: the Ideal of the Priest* by Dom Columba Marmion; from popular books like *Vessels of Clay* by Father Leo Trese, a parish priest from Michigan, to *This Way to God* by an Italian priest, Giovanni Rossi. Priestly identity was alive and well in the Catholic community, and movies like *Going My Way*, *The Keys of the Kingdom*, and *Boys Town* presented images of priests with which we could identify.

All of that has changed, and priestly identity is in something of a crisis because priestly spirituality is in something of an eclipse. In this meditation, I would like to focus on priestly identity and spirituality. To help me frame my meditation, let me begin by looking at a common spiritual-emotional problem for priests, a problem which is the very antithesis of priestly spirituality: *burnout.*

Burnout is a widespread problem, originating from overwork, physical and mental exhaustion, and over commitment on the calendar. Burnout is also a form of *inertia.* It comes, not simply from excessive activity or an overcrowded schedule, but from something far more energy-draining: the drying up of the very roots of the spiritual life and the consequent inability to perform one's priestly duties. Burnout strikes at the very roots of the priestly personality and is akin to *acedia*, described so vividly in ancient spiritual writings.

Burnout stems from a priest's failure to cultivate intimacy with God as the first priority of his priestly existence and is the direct result of the priest giving the substance of his life and person to his *work*. When the substance of the priest's life and person is given to *God*, the overflow into priestly and pastoral work is rich and nourishing, and the priest is literally inexhaustible.

This inexhaustibility is visible in the life of great priests like St. Vincent Pallotti, the apostle of Rome in the last century; St. John Bosco, John Henry Newman, Eusebio Kino, that amazing missionary of the Southwest; or those closer to us, for example, Jean Baptiste Lamy of Santa Fe, Father Flanagan of Boys Town, Bishop Fulton Sheen or Father Walter Farrell.

Burnout emerges as a weight within the soul because the roots of the spiritual life have atrophied. The only remedy is the revitalization of those roots. Communion with God, the intense cultivation of intimacy with God, is the energizing source of all genuine priestly activity. Communion with God is the *primary act* of priesthood. From this living source the work of priesthood flows, personally and pastorally; and when it is lacking, the human spirit collapses. This is precisely what happens with burnout: the priestly personality collapses from within, and the priestly spirit is drained of all energy and all joy.

The profound reason for emotional collapse is the absence of priestly contemplative prayer. The priesthood is not merely *functional*; it is essentially *ontological*. Priestly activity flows from the deep inner world of priestly identity and is nourished by union with God in prayer. The priest's identity is secured from within that intense center of his heart where the *enjoyment of God* is the very oxygen of his existence. For those who do not understand this concept they, must ultimately find the meaning of their priesthood in activity. This turn toward activity is an illusion because only when that activity is the overflow of deep intimacy with God does it nourish and enrich; without such intimacy, activity is simply a futile attempt to fill an ever-gnawing emptiness.

Unless a priest is convinced that everything vital and significant in his priesthood flows from intimacy with God, the center of his existence will be someplace else. History is full of such examples—some tragic, some humorous, and some just plain stupid. I know priests whose car or Irish Setter are more important to them than their priesthood; or some for whom hunting and fishing in Canada are more important than their availability in their parish.

Every priest must translate and interpret for himself, in the language of his own mind and culture, the divine presence that has seared Itself into the very fiber of his being. This translation and interpretation takes an effort of intellect, the assimilation of new ideas, and the cultivation of something resembling a theological *culture*. Unless a priest is convinced that the deepest part of his being has been sealed by divine love, he will seek the meaning of his priesthood in something else. *Burnout* is simply the modern version of this ancient mistake.

The priest must realize that *his* being in communion with Christ is the critical factor in pastoral work—not brilliant ideas, although these will come; not dynamic programs, although these are necessary; not the ability to organize and administer, although these qualities are essential to his work; and certainly, not the success or failure of his efforts, although hopefully these efforts will always be blessed. Joy and happiness *in God* makes the difference in priestly life and ministry. And unless joy in God burns at the very center of his existence, the priest's ultimate influence will be minimal. The old spiritual classics on priesthood tried to say this, though their language and style may not be in tune with the modern need.

Relentless priestly activity is a problem. St. Bernard of Clairvaux called it the "damnable work ethic" in his famous "Letter to Pope Eugenius III": the failure to cultivate deep, contemplative roots, exacerbated by the accompanying conviction that we are indispensable. Such beliefs can become as much a part of a priest's life as the life of a husband and father, when that man neglects his wife and children in the name of his work. This "damnable work ethic" is the masculine temptation par excellence, and priests easily succumb to it. Absorption in work can become like a drug, and the tyranny of one's daily duties—whether it is the factory, the office, or the rectory—can become a cruel taskmaster.

St. Bernard reminded Pope Eugenius that his first responsibility was to his own person, "to your mother's only son;" for if that instrument is neglected, everything else will suffer. The failure to *look to oneself* as "beloved son" is the direct cause of burnout. Once burnout takes over, any letup from work becomes a source of deep guilt until a complete loss of energy takes place, with all the dire consequences that follow.

The great tragedy of priesthood today is that everything has become, or is in danger of becoming, a mere utility—even the Eucharist. If not a utility, it becomes a naked duty, a task or obligation: to provide a spiritual service to parishioners, to fulfill a schedule, to take care of a Mass stipend or obligation. How often is Mass celebrated for the sheer joy of it, for the marvel and wonder that it is: our intimate communion with and enjoyment of the Living God? How often is celebrating Mass savored? How often do we open ourselves to its splendor and bask in its glow?

Priesthood is immersion in the Mystery of God; and the Mystery of God in which we are immersed is the Mystery of the Eucharist, the Living God in our midst, the Creator who comes into our very beings, the God who created and redeemed us and beckons us to eternal life and the wonder of His closeness. Somehow, in the battles we are fighting and the labors in which we are involved, this concept is often forgotten. The Eucharist is not a devotional exercise; it is an existential fact. Christ has sacrificed His life for us and made this love available to us in the Eucharist. Only when that truth becomes the center of our existence does our priesthood have the deep, nourishing roots it needs to gift us with happiness.

In his book on the Mass—dated, but still throbbing with a theology well worth pondering—Father Romano

Guardini wrote that, at times, we should feel banished from the altar in the face of the awesome holiness of God, painfully aware of the distance between creature and Creator. "Trust in God," he wrote, "nearness to Him and security in Him, remain thin and feeble when personal knowledge of God's exclusive majesty and awful sanctity do not counterbalance them."[1] There is something awesome and overwhelming about priestly identity and the Mysteries with which a priest is engaged. Sometimes we have to step back a bit and get a fresh perspective.

Burnout is one of the strange paradoxes of priesthood: totally unnecessary, yet a haunting reality dogging the steps of many good-willed priests and making their priestly experience a burden and a bore. When burnout happens in a marriage, a couple should go on a second honeymoon. They leave the children with relatives and go off by themselves, where they can be lovers again and recover something of the intimate relationship that brought them together. The remedy for burnout in priests is similar: a face-to-face confrontation with God in the Eucharist, in circumstances where we can savor His love and open our whole beings to Him, bask in the wonder of His love and let its awesomeness become part of our consciousness again. When that begins to happen, burnout is not only banished, it becomes impossible.

When immersion in the Mystery of God and the savoring of that Mystery becomes the very heart of priesthood, it not only transforms the life of the priest, but the lives of others as well. This is done not by what he *does* but by who he has become. That is the secret of all genuine pastoral work. Those who discover this secret very often become saints.

The basic principle of genuine priestly spirituality is this: when the heart is given to God, the *overflow* into priestly and pastoral work is inexhaustible. Such a priestly presence is constantly nourishing and enriching, for both priest and people. Now, what exactly does this mean? It means that our point of gravity is in God, in opening ourselves to Him—and no two of us will do that in quite the same way. No two saints are alike; no two priests are alike. We have to hew our own unique pathway to God; we have to cultivate and create our own priestly spirituality. We cannot be a carbon copy or a cheap imitation of someone else. I know one priest who goes to the Church at least one night a week, at midnight, and spends two hours celebrating Mass—alone. That is his way of savoring the Mystery of the Eucharist, alone with his God: *Adoro te devote, latens Deitas*. Cardinal Newman could pray only with a pen in his hand; other priests like to walk under the stars, pondering the magnitude and wonder of creation. One priest has mastered Hebrew well enough to read the Psalms in the same language in which Jesus read them. Yet another spends a week every year at a Trappist monastery, drinking in the solitude. Another priest I know exposes the Blessed Sacrament in the Church and spends an hour or two in His Presence.

Somehow, we have to nourish or recover that fascination with God, *fascinans cum Deo*, the seed and ground of our priesthood. Most of us had it at one time, but as the years went on, other things took priority. We must also remember that, during all of our priestly lives, we take the initiative; we set the pace, especially if we have been in positions of importance and authority—making decisions for others, solving problems that only we can solve, facing crises that require our authority and our particular skills. We will often be seemingly indispensable for solving massive and critical problems, with others dependent upon our action and initiative. We are critical hinges in near life-and-death situations. But that will not always be the case. The time will come when we will have to get out of the picture, when someone else will be in the driver's seat. We will no longer be needed, no longer necessary. We will be replaced. It would be tragic if the only habits we had cultivated were habits of filling important positions and making important decisions running a parish, wrapped up in duties and concerns that are essential parts of our work, but which will end when the initiative and action are no longer ours.

This change happens in the life of every priest, even bishops, and I remind myself of that. At that point, we can feel out of it, bewildered, completely lost. We could become only shadows of ourselves, surrounded by mementos of our priestly years, photos and news clippings of a full career, our total personal investment in something that is bound to pass away, perhaps bitter that we are no longer needed and that time has passed us by.

I have known priests who faced this moment gracefully and graciously, beloved and cherished in their latter years, influencing others by who they *were*, rather than by what they *did*. Such priests were venerable figures with wisdom in their eyes and deep contentment on their faces. They never considered themselves indispensable for *anything*, even though they had achieved wonders in their lifetime. They filled their golden years with the ultimate concerns that were the heart of their priesthood, and they did that with a *style* and *character* uniquely their own. *Nothing* was lost by their retiring from the scene, and they were able to recognize the differing opportunities and the very different talents that a new generation brought to their work, quick to praise that which was not their own and never looking at the past as something that belonged to them.

Those who can make this transition are the golden men, who light up their latter days with only their *presence*, giving hope and encouragement to those who come after them, their eyes on an unlimited future where they will not be present, grateful for their time on center stage as they turn their eyes to the goal of all their labors: union with God. What they have accomplished is stored away and is kept in trust where "neither moth nor decay destroys, nor thieves break in and steal" (Mt. 6:20). Knowledge of that is sufficient for them, though the whole world forgets them and they vanish from the annals of time. Their credit is kept in the only ledger that really counts.

After a lifetime of amazing and astonishing achievements, Thomas Aquinas was asked by the Lord: "Thomas, what do you ask of Me?" And his reply: "Only Thyself, Lord." He had written: "By loving God, we glow to gaze on His beauty." And again: "Our conversation with God is through contemplation. The Holy Spirit makes us God's lovers." And still again: "The highest perfection of human life consists in the mind of man being open to God." Then, this remarkable statement:

> Human perfection consists of intimacy with
> God and so it is most proper that with all

31

that is in him, and with all the powers of his being, a man should penetrate Divine things and be wholly occupied with them; so that his mind is absorbed in contemplation and his reasoning powers in the exploration of those things that are of God.[2]

Some of these truths articulated by St. Thomas are perhaps a little beyond most of us, though they point to what our priestly existence is really all about. We are the dispensers of the Mysteries of God, and it is only fitting and proper that we should be deeply immersed in those Mysteries, which define our own priestly existence. The prime fact of the Christian faith is that the incomprehensible God wants to embrace us in a communion of love, and from the plenitude of that love heals and saves us. The priest is the living instrument of this communion and is placed at the deepest level of this communion with the Godhead by his very vocation. Immersion in the Mystery of God defines him as a human person, and in and through this communion, he touches the lives of others.

# Notes

1    Romano Guardini, *Meditations Before Mass* (Manchester: Sophia Institute Press, 1993), 50.
2    St. Thomas Aquinas, *De Perfectione Spirtualis Vitae*, Marietta Edition, Turin, Italy, in *Opuscula Theological*, 1954.

# Works Cited

Bolton, Herbert Eugene. *The Padre on Horseback* (Chicago: Loyola University Press, 1963).

Chautard, O.C.S.O, Dom Jean Baptiste. *The Soul of the Apostolate* (Trappist, KY: Abbey of Gethsemani, 1946).

Guardini, Romano. *Meditations Before Mass*, republished as *Preparation for Mass* by Sophia Institute Press, Manchester, N.H.. 1997.

Horgan, Paul. *Lamy of Santa Fe* (New York: Farrar, Straus & Giroux, 1975).

Kerr, Ian. *John Henry Newman* ( Oxford University Press, 1988).

Marmion, O.S.B, Dom Columba. *Christ the Ideal of the Priest* ( San Francisco: Ignatius, 2205).

Phelan, E.B. *Don Bosco: A Spritiual Portrait* (Garden City, NY: Doubleday, 1963).

Reeves, Thomas C. *America's Bishop: The Life and Times of Fulton J. Sheen* (San Francisco: Encounter Books, 2001).

Stevens, Clifford. *Father Flanagan: Builder of Boys* (New York: PJ. Kenedy & Sons, 1967).

Trese, Leo. *Vessels of Clay* (New York: Sheed & Ward, 1946).

St. Bernard of Clairvaux, *De Consideratione* II, 2.

St. Thomas Aquinas, *Commentary on the Divine Names*.
--*Summa Contra Gentiles*, IV, 22.
--*Summa Contra Gentiles*, III, 130.
--*De Perfectione Spirtualis Vitae*, Marietta Edition, Turin, Italy, in *Opuscula Theological*, 1954.

# The Call of Celibacy

The question of celibacy is forefront in the public mind, and those who have no knowledge of this ancient discipline, and no real interest, often wax eloquent on the subject, as if God Himself had consulted them on the matter. I have often felt that the less said about one's choice of celibacy, the better, since it is a choice born in the silence of one's relationship with God. None of us can really put into words the reasons for saying "yes" to that choice. But we have to talk about it, if only to stabilize the vocation in those who have chosen it and to give assurances to young priests and seminarians of the validity of their choice and the validity of the vocation itself, particularly in these days when sacred veils are being torn off the holiest of things and prying minds do not hesitate to question so long and so sacred a tradition.

Celibacy is chosen for deep, personal reasons that cannot always be expressed. Based on the wonder of God and the magnitude of eternal life, celibacy is bound up with a fascination for the holy. It is a vocation with hidden springs deep in the recesses of the soul: private, personal, sacred, and open to the gaze of no one but God Himself. Celibacy is a choice born of solitude, where a personal encounter with God takes place, much as married couples choose *mutual solitude* as a result of their falling in love with one another. The man who chooses celibacy may not be able to articulate it as a concept, but he gravitates, in his most prayerful moments, to a meeting with his Maker that defines his whole existence. A priest's solitude is one that he does not inhabit alone.

Celibacy is chosen freely, in the innocence of a personal experience with God, without, at the same time, bothering to work out all of the implications of that choice. Usually, the choice of celibacy has already been made when practical questions about living celibacy start to be considered. At that point, it is simply a matter of making *explicit* what was *implicit* in that choice and discovering the fruitfulness of a celibate vocation.

Celibacy is a very delicate matter, so highly personal that no one should enter into the depths of what motivates this choice without being invited. A young man discovers that his choice of celibacy springs from the deep wells of his own motivation, from the deep personal threads of his own inner self, where he said, "Yes," to God. When these threads are beheld as a complete fabric, then a vocation can be stabilized. This beholding is usually accomplished in prayerful spiritual direction.

What is affirmed in the choice of celibacy is as highly personal and as sacred in its intimacy as the intimacies of marriage. It is bound up with that deep personal relationship that each human being has with his Creator. *The choice of celibacy is the living language in which a man expresses this relationship*, and it is a language of affirmation. Seeing that celibacy is an affirmation and not a negation is critical to the whole meaning of the vocation.

When a young priest or seminarian discovers the roots of his own motivation for becoming a priest, he is faced with the awesomeness of his choice and the wonder of a personal experience of God that led to that choice. Celibacy, then, is not seen as the taking upon oneself of a pattern of life dictated by someone else or the imposition by some higher authority of a way of life to which he has not consented. Rather, celibacy is a living expression of the thrust of his whole being toward God and the living language in which he clothes his own experience of God.

The vocation may have been *given* in the darkness and obscurity of a budding adolescence, with that mixture of motivation and feelings that are a part of young love; but it is *chosen* in the full-faced recognition of the Beloved. Like each individual marriage, each vocation to celibacy is something totally original, arising from the dialogue between man and God and bears the stamp of a particular individual with his wealth of personal experience and unique history.

Ultimately, the *implicit* choice of celibacy must be made *explicit* through thought, reflection, and self-knowledge. Unless celibacy is seen as more than the foregoing of the intimacies of marriage, as the whole world around us seems to think, the splendor and grandeur of the vocation will not be grasped. Rather, it will be buried in reflections unrelated to the reality of celibacy as an intimacy with God that defines and embodies the very nature of priesthood itself.

Celibacy, for the priest, is intimacy with God not because marriage is an obstacle to this intimacy with God but because celibacy provides that *total, personal solitude from which the priest can cultivate an exclusive love of God.* His vocation is to bear witness to the overpowering reality of God. His celibacy does not so much bear witness to the *absence* of sex in his life, even though it includes this absence, but is primarily a symbol of his total consecration to *the presence* of God and eternal things. Therefore, his celibacy flows from an exuberance of love—which sets the tone for his entire vocation.

Therefore, celibacy is not simply a denial; it is also an *affirmation*, an affirmation of realities beyond the human and beyond this world. We ought not to wonder that its sublime nature is not grasped by those whose horizons are limited to this world. The passion that is quickened in the spirit and mind of the celibate reaches beyond the roots of manhood; the joy he experiences wraps his whole existence in wonder, and the Mystery that he shares begins to reveal an incredible and extraordinary relationship which is the very foundation of this universe and is the basic charter of humanity itself. We are created for God and eternity. The celibacy of the Catholic priest proclaims this to the world.

The *specific excellence* of celibacy, then, consists in the *personal solitude* provided by celibacy, enabling the celibate priest to cultivate an exclusive intimacy with God. The priest's *cultivation* of intimacy with God as his chief preoccupation is the specific fruit of celibacy. This reveals, contrary to a common impression, that celibacy is not merely a physiological state, the mere fact that the celibate *sleeps alone*. The personal solitude of celibacy is the condition for the possibility of cultivating intimacy with God.

Much insight on the topic of celibacy has emerged from Pope John Paul II's *Theology of the Body*. The Pope recovered certain concepts that were lost in Catholic theology for centuries and gave them a new context, rehabilitating them for a new generation of Catholics, and drawing out their startling significance for his new evangelization. One of those concepts is *fascination with God* as the root reality of the vocation to celibacy, founding it, not on a juridical decree or canonical imperative, but solely on the wonder of God, which blossoms in so many beautiful ways in the priesthood and consecrated life.

Fascination with God cannot be fully explained any more than a man can fully explain his fascination with the woman he is going to marry. No judicial decree compels a man to marry, though laws govern marriage and responsibilities flow from it. Genuine celibacy is based solely on this *fascination with God*, even though it, like marriage, is governed by certain laws and carries with it certain obligations.

As the Pope stated so clearly in his *Theology of the Body*, celibacy, like intimacy in marriage, is a form of self-giving, not in the sense of a self-denying, self-immolation, but in the sense of opening one's whole being to the wonder of God and of His splendor. We need only reflect on what we do every time we stand at the altar to grasp the dignity of our call to celibacy and its origin in our own wonder at God's holiness.

> Godhead here in hiding, Whom I do adore,
> Masked by these bare shadows, shape and nothing more,
> See, Lord, at Thy service, low lies here a heart,
> Lost, all lost in wonder, at the God Thou art.[1]

Communion with God, the cultivation of intimacy with God, is the immediate goal and energizing source of all genuine priestly spirituality. Thus, the primary act of priesthood must be prayer. From this living source, the work of priesthood flows, personally and pastorally. When this communion with God is lacking, the human spirit collapses into burnout, a form of inertia. This truth must be repeated in any discussion of the vocation to celibacy. Celibacy is more than the *absence* of a spouse or a carefully safeguarded chastity. Rooted in *magnificence*, possessing an exuberance in living, and bursting the bonds of the ordinary by reaching to the extraordinary, much in the priesthood proceeds from the glowing center of celibacy.

We are not mystics in monasteries, cultivating a corporate solitude apart from the normal concerns and activities of life. Monks and nuns live in this kind of solitude, but the personal solitude of celibacy does not require this physical solitude. Celibacy itself is the solitude. The celibate fastens his attention and affection on God—breathing, eating, drinking God, in a sense, and inhabiting a vast and beautiful aloneness where the thought of God can be nurtured.

We have been personally called by God to this priestly vocation, and the hand of God is upon us every step of the way. God calls a definite human being, a man, a member of the male sex, with a unique, distinct, and specific personal background and history; we have been called to labor for Him in a definite time and place. This living consciousness of the hand of God upon us personally gives our vocation its confidence, its strength, its creative power, and its possibilities. We return to this consciousness again and again, whenever discouragement enters our hearts. We are not volunteers in a great army of priests: faceless, anonymous, with lock-step marching orders like the soldiers of Sparta, void of personality or initiative of our own. We are living instruments in the hands of Jesus Christ to carry on His work, and we cannot afford to let any kind of discouragement make us forget this.

I want to briefly address the scandals that have rocked the Church in the United States and elsewhere, draining enthusiasm and hope from the lives of many priests, especially as these scandals multiply. I cannot understand how any man, with the oil of ordination on his hands, could betray everything that his priesthood stands for in such a way; I cannot fathom the moral corruption, depravity, and total disregard for the welfare of others, bound up in that depravity. The only conclusion I can arrive at is that this deep vice establishes a foothold in a priest's life, turns it into a propensity, and then becomes a horrible habit. The danger is that we will be so shocked and shaken by these horrendous examples of unpriestly conduct that there will be an eclipse in our minds and spirits of the vocation to which we have been called and the powerful link with Jesus Christ that *is* our priesthood. That vision of human depravity can blot out every priestly instinct fashioned by years of formation.

Alexander Pope, the English poet, has a graphic commentary on how this depravity begins to take over the mind and heart of a man. His words are worth pondering as the mystery of this kind of unpriestly behavior rises up in our minds. Pope says:

> Vice is a monster of so frightful mien,
> That to be hated, needs but to be seen
> But seen too oft, familiar with her face,
> We first endure, then pity ... then embrace.[2]

41

Shocking as the scandals are, these examples of priestly depravity are not what we should have in our minds. Instead, we should hold in our minds exemplars of priesthood: Maximilian Kolbe, Jerzy Popieluszko, Father Flanagan, Fulton Sheen, Vincent Pallotti, and countless others. In the crisis that is upon us, we must realize and insist that celibacy can be joyfully lived if a man retains and deepens his spiritual life, courageously seeking the truth about himself and any emotional/moral healing that is appropriate.

Looked upon chiefly as a deprivation by popular culture, the true meaning of celibacy is found in the personal solitude that celibacy provides. Such solitude becomes the arena for the priest's intimacy with God. The celibate life demands a regular portion of prayerful solitude, and the cultivation of this solitude is the most fundamental skill the priest must acquire. He lives, he seeks God, he thinks, and he labors from a place of personal solitude defined by prayer.

As noted above, this solitude does not exist for its own sake, and it is possible to fill it with the most trivial of occupations. It exists to provide the priest with an environment where intimacy with God can be cultivated with passion. In this, the celibate is not unlike the married man. Marriage provides a common life for a man and woman in which intimacy can be cultivated and experienced. Married couples *live alone*; they leave father and mother so they can cleave to each other and become "one flesh." Without this common life of married solitude, the deepest and most meaningful intimacy in their relationship would be diminished or rendered impossible to achieve.

The personal solitude of celibacy gives the priest a *common life* with God where intimacy with God can be cultivated. Many young priests complete seminary without the faintest idea of what to do with all that personal solitude. Perhaps they have never been told that the very purpose of their celibate condition is to provide solitude where their intimate life with God can be cultivated.

In this day of television and its hundreds of channels, with the computer and Internet where a man can spend hours unaware of how the time is passing; in this day of easy mobility and the distractions of any large city, solitude is constantly invaded. All the more reason to insist upon it. We must take up this cross daily—resisting anything that invades the space reserved for God alone.

Ultimately then, the celibate priest is not *alone* in his solitude, even though he sacrificed the life of sacramental marriage. If that solitude is entered well, he can cultivate an intimacy with God beyond what I can describe. The theological foundation of celibacy is that we are created for beatitude, for perfect and total happiness, for the full and overflowing possession of the life of God. Everything earthly and human only mirrors the reality of eternal life, and everything in human life has been touched by the beauty of God and reflects something of His greatness and His being.

Marriage and human love are one of the loveliest expressions of God's goodness, and the beatitude of married love is a true anticipation of that final beatitude. The priest does not empty his life of marriage and a love for another as the first act in saying "yes" to a celibate life; this is a reflex action. Instead, he takes a step first *toward the joy* he experiences in intimacy with God.

This aspect of celibacy is important to emphasize, for there is no hint in true celibacy of an objection to married friendship or a negative attitude toward married beatitude. But *the sacrifice of married happiness is not less for all that*, and the personal significance of this sacrifice should not be underestimated. The celibate deprives himself of the crowning act of his manhood. If that vacuum is not filled with something that carries joy at his very roots, the deprivation and emptiness will be almost too much to bear. This is a consequence of celibacy that has not often been touched upon, which explains some of the strange aberrations in clerical life and some tragic consequences of an ill-motivated and immature commitment to celibacy.

For the priest, solitude is freedom in the highest degree: a spiritual adventure that engages him at the very depths of his being. The solitary life can be harrowing and lonely because of a man's own emotional emptiness and a lack of intimate companionship. But it can also be tremendously satisfying as new horizons with God are glimpsed and the marvel and wonder of God become more real. Celibates, since they are basically contemplatives, have always had a passion for solitude. Filling this solitude with prayer becomes the symbol and crown of their celibate consecration, so that solitude with God becomes the very breath of life for them.

In the mutual solitude of marriage, the partners turn toward each other. They begin to unveil and reveal to each other a secret face and a private self that they reveal to no one else. They begin to cultivate an intimacy with each other that is the very foundation of their relationship. This intimacy is the living embodiment of their attraction for each other. In the solitude of celibacy, the celibate turns toward God and opens all his being to God's splendor. He begins to cultivate an intimacy that is the root reason for his existence. The solitude itself does not provide this—it merely provides the opportunity. Intimacy with God is chosen by the celibate himself.

In the sacrament of marriage, the act of marrying does not itself provide a common life for the couple. They have to make plans for the future, find a house for themselves, and fill it with all of the elements of proprietorship that make it truly their own. It must be personal and private, and their very desire to live together and cultivate their love for each other makes setting up their home very exciting. The priest, too, if his celibacy is genuine, wants to create conditions where he can live in the presence of God, turning his face more and more to God, unbarring to Him his deepest self, shown only to God.

The scientist needs his laboratory; the artist, his studio; the musician, his conservatory; even the child, his playground. Every art and specialty, every skill and pursuit, needs an appropriate environment. The artist without his studio and the scientist without his laboratory simply could not create their works of beauty or their works of the mind, and the human race would be impoverished as a consequence. Their work proceeds from a certain kind of *intimacy*, and without it, the world is deprived of the beauty of their insight. The celibate priest also needs his solitude, but it must be a solitude where the tools and the nourishment for his intimacy with God give him his own unique *culture*, his own *civilization*, where he breathes a different kind of air and sings a different kind of song. The windows of this *culture* must open to eternity so he can keep his face continuously pressed against the windowpane of God.

Being alone is not enough; the aloneness must be filled. Filling the aloneness with God is the exciting thing about being a celibate. The celibate priest in his prayerful solitude must create this kind of habitation of the spirit: where insight abounds, where intuition is sparked, where ideas flourish, and where breathing spaces for the Spirit are discovered.

# Notes

1    St. Thomas Aquinas, *Adoro Te Devote*, trans. Gerard Manley Hopkins, SJ, found in *Manual of Prayers*, compiled by Father James D. Watkins (Woodridge, IL: Midwest Theological Forum, 2005), 376.

2    Alexander Pope, *The works of Alexander Pope, with notes and illustrations, by himself and others,* vol. 4, ed. William Roscoe (London: Oxford University Press, 1847), 77.

# Works Cited

Pope, Alexander. *The works of Alexander Pope, with notes and illustrations, by himself and others,* vol. 4, ed. William Roscoe (London: Oxford University Press, 1847).

Pope John Paul II, *Theology of the Body: Human Love in the Divine Plan* (Boston: Pauline Media & Books, 1997).

St. Thomas Aquinas, *Adoro Te Devote*, trans. Gerard Manley Hopkins, SJ, found in *Manual of Prayers*, compiled by Father James D. Watkins (Woodridge, IL: Midwest Theological Forum, 2005).

# What Does it Mean to Be a Priest?

George Weigel's biography of Pope John Paul II, entitled *Witness to Hope*, is a massive volume revealing achievements of the Pope that have scarcely been talked about and many battles he fought as priest, bishop, and pope to further the work of Jesus Christ. A sense of a personal providence struck me in reading the book, as well as a strong, unyielding, and dynamic vision of priesthood that Pope John Paul II carried with him from his first days as a seminarian in the secret, underground seminary established by the Cardinal Archbishop of Krakow during the Nazi occupation of Poland. He hammered out that vision of priesthood in dangerous and difficult times, with dangers to his own life, as he worked out the implications of his vocation with the Nazi terror surrounding him.

We can miss the weight of what a vocation to the priesthood really means. For priests like Karol Wojtyla and Maximilian Kolbe, the vocation was lived in the most difficult of circumstances. With an unwavering conviction that God was giving constant support every step of the way, both men entered into the true meaning of their priestly vocation.

Pope John Paul II's example and words have shown us the fantastic possibilities of priesthood. He has said, in substance, to each of us, whatever our assignment, whatever our role in the Church, that our only limitations are our own efforts. We are commissioned to create the future. Do we recognize the priesthood as a vocation given to men grasped by God, or do we see ourselves as just another name in the diocesan directory? The vocation to priesthood is a marvel and a mystery, and no priest can escape the reality of God deeply penetrating and affecting his total personality. Every priest, from the day he is ordained, senses a burning at the center of his being. As a priest attends to a multitude of priestly tasks, he realizes, if he has pondered his priesthood well, that what he *does* is not half as important as who he *is*. Rather, who he *is* communicates to his people much more than what he *does*.

The life of the priest, however, includes a *doing*, a task, and his priesthood is more than the complex of ritual and sacramental events comprising his daily routine. The work of the priesthood is a uniquely *theological* task, involving the cultivation of the identity of human beings, an identity which links them to an eternal and transcendent God. Men and women are more than inhabitants of the earth; their substance reaches beyond the limits of their earthly personality. Priestly and pastoral work is uniquely theological. By his example, Pope John Paul II taught us to keep our eyes fixed on the eternal goals of the priestly tasks—even through the most harrowing circumstances that a man can face.

The creative possibilities of a vibrant and luminous priesthood are absolutely unlimited. This unlimited possibility presupposes that *the priest is living at the deepest level of his being,* receptive to the intense furnace of thought and insight where something resembling genius is born. There are no patterns for priestly effectiveness; there are no absolute models for pastoral theology. Every priest, in a sense, is in a land without any maps. He is in uncharted territory; and although the living example of the great priests who have gone before him can give inspiration and encouragement, the creative art of his work must be his own.

Pope John Paul II has demonstrated that the priest's involvement in the pastoral task is only by way of *overflow*. He further evidenced this by spending an hour before the Blessed Sacrament prior to celebrating Mass; and as Cardinal Archbishop of Krakow, he did his pastoral planning at a desk in his episcopal chapel. The very genius of pastoral work depends upon its flowing from a deep intimacy with God, and this intimacy is the very foundation of priestly lifestyle and an exhilarating source of joy. Joy in God is at the very heart of priesthood, as joy in each other is at the very heart of marriage.

In marriage, the intimacy of the couple in their mutual solitude creates a conjugal paradise; from this intimate center and their continual experience of this intimacy, the couple builds the home, the family, and the many activities of that family. From the priest's own solitude, he cultivates and experiences intimacy with God, the priestly paradise, from which the whole work of priesthood proceeds. As the intimacy of marriage produces the fruit of children, the priest's intimacy with God produces life in the priest's own soul—a life that informs his entire pastoral ministry.

What is the Church's ministry as we settle into the twenty first century? What is the Church in an age of atoms and terror, in an age of ballistic missiles and the rapidity of Internet communications, in an age of expanding education and political unrest? Pope John Paul II felt he had to deepen the pastoral mission of the Church and reexamine every element of that mission for a new age. He called for a new evangelization, and before he died, he began to draft the blueprint for that evangelization.

In talk after talk, in document after document, John Paul II spoke especially to those who doubted the meaning or value of priestly service. His effort was to reinvigorate the priesthood and restore morale to priests throughout the world. Pope John Paul II saw a basic rupture between creature and Creator, both in the priesthood and in marriage, as well as in basic human affairs. He exerted immense effort to repair that rupture—first of all, in the lives of priests, who carry on the mission of the Church in every city and nation, in every town and village, and in every human habitation scattered across the face of the world.

In his sexual ethic, Pope John Paul II sought to liberate a genuine and purified *eros* for the full and mature spontaneity that finds its fulfillment in self-giving. In his pastoral ethic, he endeavored to liberate the priestly *ethos* for a full and mature spontaneity that finds its fulfillment in works of spiritual insight that transform and enrich the lives of the Christian people. The priest's life, through consecrated celibacy, becomes the means for an exclusive intimacy with God. This gift of self, freely offered and freely received, becomes the instrument for the evangelization of the whole world through the formation of the laity.

The burning center of the priest's effectiveness is his own intimacy with God. This intense center of the priest's existence has sparked pastoral genius from the very beginnings of Christianity: the Scriptural genius of Origen, the mystical-pastoral genius of St. Basil of Caesarea, the contemplative genius of St. Bruno, the missionary genius of St. Boniface, the cultural genius of Celtic monasticism, the social genius of the Jesuit Reductions in Paraguay, the theological genius of St. Thomas Aquinas, the pastoral genius of Pope John Paul II. The horizon of priesthood is endless, and the future will certainly hold surprises for the Church—and the world—as monumental and significant as any of the past.

The greatest mistake of priestly work is to imagine that the mere management of resources, financial or otherwise, is the key problem and critical burden of the pastoral task. This has never been true. The critical factor in priestly work is the priest's own intimacy with God. From this glowing center, everything vital and viable flows. The very roots of the priest's psychology must be immersed in a happiness that comes from intimacy with God. Failing to learn this lesson is to remain a child playing with his toys and never know the kiss of God, which must be indelibly seared into the living flesh of our deepest self.

The priest is a man immersed in the mystery of God, a mystery that serves as the groundwork of human existence and defines his personality and his task. From the depths of his own communion with God, the priest works. Everything *significant* in his work flows from his union with the mystery of Jesus Christ, the living embodiment of God in human form. The priest is drawn into the deepest level of communion with the Trinity. This is the true meaning of priesthood: sharing in Christ's sanctifying mission as bridegroom and head: a mission born of the cross. The reality of the priest's sharing in Christ's own mission is not only the

root of priestly effectiveness, but the means by which vocations to the priesthood should be fostered. The vocation
to the priesthood is born in the depths of an experience of
God. From the depths of that experience, the vocation grows
and blossoms.

We cannot really explain the vocation to priesthood.
It is bound up with the mystery of God, which we simply
cannot fathom. No amount of personal investigation can
fully uncover the personal roots of the vocation itself. But
there is no doubt about *how* the vocation is born: from an
experience of God which moves a man's personal relationship with God established at Baptism to a totally new depth.
It is an intimacy with God that beckons from the depths of
the priestly mission of Christ the Bridegroom.

Every priest worthy of his title will admit that he
craved this intimacy with God from the first moment the
thought of the priesthood entered his mind. This is a golden
moment, never to be forgotten. This intimacy, this communion with God, is the first act and driving force of priestly
existence, and when *that* is forgotten the vocation becomes a
harrowing emotional and spiritual vacuum. Father Karl Rahner, one of the most profound thinkers of our time, wrote:

> The Christian of the future will be a mystic
> or he will not exist at all ... if by mysticism we
> mean, not singular parapsychological phe-
> nomena, but a genuine experience of God
> emerging from the heart of our existence,
> this statement is very true, and its truth and
> importance will become still clearer in the
> spirituality of the future.[1]

If what Father Rahner said is true of the Christian of the future, it is more certainly true for the priest of the future. We do not elicit vocations to the priesthood by appeals to service to the common good or works of justice and charity. The attraction to the priesthood is, first of all, an attraction for God and for intimacy with Him. Some men may first be attracted to priesthood to "serve" but only those who allow Christ to heal, love, and inhabit them will ever be what Christ fully intended in their call: bridegrooms living to sacrifice their lives for the spiritual welfare of the Church out of a deep and continual receiving of divine love in and through the Eucharist. From this glowing center, the works of priesthood proceed.

When the substance of a man is given to God, rooted in the intimacy which is the beginning of all priestly joy, the overflow into the pastoral ministry is inexhaustible. When the priest reverses that equation and focuses upon himself, he lays the seeds for discouragement, which seems to be so much a part of the priesthood today. Pope John Paul II was trying to communicate to the priests of the third millennium what might be called *epic* priesthood: great priests transforming the world around them, life for others flows from the depths of their inner prayer. When this epic quality is at work, remarkable things begin to happen, and the possessors of such deep interiority become saints.

Something innate in the nature of priesthood, when permitted its full sway, transforms whole nations, peoples, parishes, and dioceses, and sets up a circle of influence that lasts for centuries. The preservation and enlivening of this epic quality of priesthood is what Pope John Paul II had in mind and which assures the individual priest that he can truly be, "the salt of the earth" and "the light of the world" (Mt. 5:13-14). When everything to which the priest puts his hand proceeds from that deep world of interiority where he communes with his God, his priesthood transcends the reality of his human limitations.

# Notes

1     Karl Rahner, SJ, *The Spirituality of the Church of the Future,* in *Theological Investigations,* Volume XX, (New York: Crossroad Publishing Company, 1986), 149.

# Works Cited

Karl Rahner, SJ, *The Spirituality of the Church of the Future,* in *Theological Investigations,* Volume XX (New York: Crossroad Publishing Company, 1986).

George Weigel, *Witness to Hope* (Cliff Street Books, Harper/Collins, 1999).

*Gaudium et Spes: Pastoral Constitution on the Church in the Modern World,* Second Vatican Council, 1965.

# Faith and Fearlessness

One of the most important things we can bring to our priestly work is originality, tapping the great world of the Word of God in fresh ways for the current age. This living contact with our heritage of faith should be evident in every word we speak from the pulpit and in the enthusiasm with which we go about our work. Whether we know it or not, we are the apples of God's eye, and He watches over each of us with tender and loving care. We cannot get a sense of that care simply from intermittent spiritual reading: we must have continual contact with the Word. The faith must become vision, and a sense of God's personal providence should influence our affective and intellectual powers. The ancient Irish monks, those luminous bearers of the Gospel to the emerging cultures of Europe, had a sense of God and never lost the knowledge of His constant care and attention:

> They heard His voice above the ocean's roar,
> They felt His touch in every wind that blew,
> And from out that vast Eternity He dwelt in,
> He called to them as lovers to come home.[1]

Our call to the priesthood is ultimately a call to eternal life, a call to us personally and individually; the priesthood is not merely a call to service here and now. We must not allow practical problems, critical decisions, and pastoral planning to blot out the vision of our final goal. In the western world, we are so immersed in the practical and the immediate, in comfort and convenience, in performance and efficiency, that our link with the eternal and transcendent God can easily be eclipsed. That is the reason for much of the depression, disappointment, and discouragement that we experience.

The mind is a precious commodity, especially for a priest; and the Church encourages the cultivation of the mind by recognizing new Doctors of the Church. Faith is, first of all, a gift to the mind, knowledge that we could not possibly have except as a gift. The luminous words of St. Thomas Aquinas at the beginning of the *Summa Theologiae* describe theology, the science of the faith, as the "wisdom above all human wisdoms," and explain that the study of this wisdom is "sublime, useful, and delightful." Father Walter Farrell speaks of "sanctity of the intellect" as an indispensable endowment of priests. We go to God on the two wings of Wisdom and Love, and neither can be neglected if we are to be the "salt of the earth" and "light of the world" (Mt. 5:13-14).

The young Father Karol Wojtyla, for his doctoral dissertation at the *Angelicum* in Rome in 1947, wrote a remarkable study of faith, which opens windows upon the question of priestly spirituality. He demonstrates that faith is not merely the assent to certain doctrines and teachings, as a mere intellectual exercise, but a personal encounter with the living God. The object of faith is not a list of statements and propositions but God Himself, in whom the believer transcends the boundaries of earthly existence in a living encounter with the Author of faith. This personal encounter with the living God is the root and foundation of the mutual self-giving that is the very heart of the priesthood itself and of the vocation to celibacy, as this pope understood it.

By faith, we begin to know and experience God as a *Person*. The two-volume collection containing parts of the *Summa Theologiae*, called *Basic Writings of St. Thomas Aquinas*, is worth taking the time to read. The first article of the collection asks: "Whether the Object of Faith is the First Truth?" In this remarkable article, St. Thomas states that faith is a direct contact with God and that such contact is the beginning of our spiritual life, which will culminate in the very possession of God in eternity. Cultivation of this faith and this encounter with God is critical. We cannot and must not be satisfied with a mere "notional assent" to statements of faith. Instead, we must develop our faith into a "real assent," the earth-shaking implications of that assent in the practical expression of priestly life.

Theology is born from faith. It bursts from a heart and mind so in love with the mystery of God that one must articulate, express, and give voice to this mystery. Studying theology is much more than simply obtaining a degree. Theology originates from a living encounter with God, an encounter that is the hallmark of priestly existence. Degrees in theology are important, but the *habitus* of theology, as St. Thomas understood it, should be the personal achievement and endowment of every priest, if he is to be a true "steward of the mysteries of God" to his people (1 Cor. 4:1). Do we spend more time with popular media than we do with the classics of theology? Not that we should neglect knowledge of the world in which we live and the events that shape our world, but we should also be in living contact with our heritage of faith, in all its depth and scope, so that we can continually break open the bread of the Word for those we serve.

We must never forget that we are pilgrims, still on a journey, and faith illumines every step of the way. Faith must be, first of all, a personal journey, a personal exploration of God, a personal savoring of God, and a personal expectation of the possession of God for all eternity. St. Thomas has a remarkable statement, not found in his massive theological writings but in a study of the *Divine Names*, one of his most contemplative works:

> He speaks of the seeker of God, not merely learning about Divine things, but also experiencing them.... This does not come from a mere intellectual acquaintance with the terms of scientific theology, but from loving the things of God and cleaving to them by affection.[2]

Is this for mystics in monasteries rather than priests in parishes? Is this pre-occupation with the things of God beyond our capability and completely out of touch with the practical circumstances of our priestly and pastoral existence? God forbid that anyone should think so. Would the scandals that have rocked the priesthood have happened if the things of God were the main preoccupation of the lives of those priests? We must explore, emphasize, and return to the contemplative side of our priesthood, the uniquely *Levitical* dimension of our priesthood, for the strength, nourishment, and enrichment we need to be apostles and heralds of the new evangelization.

Faith, it is true, is a certain darkness, for it is not our natural environment. We must receive new eyes and new senses to make our way on the journey that leads to eternal life. We do not possess the pure intellects of the angels, and so we must grope our way, push boldly forward in spite of the darkness and obscurity; then, we begin to live by that theological vision that comes from such an effort. In time, we become luminous ourselves, bearers of light to a darkened world and to every person whose life we have touched.

Is this not why people look to us? They desire something more than a mere observer of the human scene, a commentator on the politics of the day, or the bearer of the latest news. *We can be men with our feet firmly grounded in this world but with our minds concentrated upon the mystery of God.* Though this image of the priest may have disappeared from sight, it can be recovered. We must be pastorally astute and administratively competent; the times demand no less of us. However, unless we become visionaries and mystics, poets and dreamers, we will be nothing but hirelings in our ministry, the unprofitable servant who wasted his master's patrimony. Can we allow ourselves to become so immersed in the business of running a parish or office that we forget the very purpose of that parish or office? That has happened hundreds, if not thousands, of times, and we are not immune to that most insidious of temptations. The bright window of faith can easily become tarnished—and we can scarcely notice it.

A remarkable saint, little known these days, who had a powerful effect upon thinking on these matters, is St. Antoninus of Florence. He lived in the bustling and mercantile city of Florence, Italy, in the days of the Medici, when profit was the chief business of the city's life. He wrote a famous book of moral theology, which considered the issue of wealth—making wealth, piling up of wealth, purpose of wealth. He arrived at some remarkable conclusions, straight out of the Gospels, but seldom mentioned these days when CEOs and corporate executives require huge salaries and bonuses and when the whole country is focused on the daily stock reports.

Wealth is a gift of God, says St. Antoninus, and its purpose is to enable a man to care for his family, free from anxiety about the future. Living in such contentment facilitates dialogue and communion with his Maker. St. Antoninus was not speaking about priests; he was speaking about fathers of families, businessmen, corporate executives, merchants, farmers, and factory workers. The purpose of making and having money is not mere social security. Rather, social security itself has a further purpose: the freedom to enter into and remain in relationship with his Maker. Money, wealth, and the possession of wealth are at the service of a contemplative preoccupation with God and eternity—a remarkable conclusion. Too many books on Catholic social doctrine stop at freedom from poverty—mere social and economic justice—without considering the ultimate purpose of this freedom.

Considering all of these things, a priest's theological study should continue throughout his whole life, and every Church document on priesthood has stressed this concept. Reading to know the bare bones of a doctrine or to quote a Council decree or official statement is not enough. We must nourish our own mind on this vast heritage of Truth; those of us who are able to do so should not be unfamiliar with the great minds of the Church—ancient, medieval, and modern. For as every great theological mind has admitted, from the early Fathers of the Church to Benedict XVI, theology can create openings for adventures of the mind and heart if we courageously embark on them. Pope John XXIII, who is not known for his intellectual achievements, was deeply versed in the Fathers and Doctors of the Church and possessed the capacity to apply the Gospel to the concrete situations of daily life and work. His words on this duty and ability to communicate to the modern world the vision of the Gospel and the need for pondering that Gospel continuously are quite surprising:

> There is no other possible path except ... to say, as if for the first time, what has nevertheless been said, and to repeat unremittingly, what has never been said: to plunge into the inexhaustible hidden treasures of Holy Scripture, to take them up again, to restate them, and make them appear fresh and new, since the novelty is not in what is said, but in seeing it again in a new light.[3]

# Notes

1    Reverend Clifford Stevens, *The Harp of Brenach* (New York: Jay Street Publishing Co., 2004).
2    St. Thomas Aquinas, *Commentary on the Divine Names*, 11, 4, 191.
3    Giancarlo Zizola, *The Utopia of Pope John XXIII* (New York: Orbis, 1979).

# Works Cited

*Basic Writings of St. Thomas Aquinas*, ed. Anton C. Pegis (New York: Random House, 1945).

Jarrett, O.P., Bede. *St. Antoninus and Mediaevil Economics* (St. Louis: B. Herder, 1914).

St. Thomas Aquinas. *Commentary on the Divine Names*, 11, 4, 191

Stevens, Reverend Clifford. *The Harp of Brenach* (New York: Jay Street Publishing Co., 2004).

Wojtyla, Karol. *Faith According to Saint John of the Cross* , trans. Jordan Aumann, O.P. (San Francisco: Ignatius Press, 1981).

Giancarlo Zizola, *The Utopia of Pope John XXIII* (New York: Orbis, 1979).

# Hope and Fidelity

What does it mean to be a priest of hope in these times of illusion and false prophets? The world needs our hope: in the midst of dangerous world conflicts, the violence and terror that we hear about every day; in the midst of a pagan and secular society where almost anything goes; in the midst of broken marriages and family crises; in the midst of corporate crime in high places; in the midst of the scandals that have shaken the Church. Concentrating only upon these examples, bewailing them as indicative of the full truth of our time, is a great danger. Perhaps we will begin to feel that God has deserted His world. Whether we like it or not, *this* is the world redeemed by Jesus Christ, and *this* is the world to which we are commissioned to bring hope and cheer—the promise of the Gospel of Jesus Christ. We should be living examples of His hope, His cheerfulness, and His promise. Fashioned and chosen by Jesus Christ to bring the Good News of Jesus Christ to the world, *our* world, we should be infused with joy beyond all understanding and hope that cannot be submerged by suffering.

We can easily feel sorry for ourselves considering the problems, difficulties, and decisions we have to make, failing to see how graciously, generously, and lavishly we are personally blessed by God. No one should be able to steal this blessedness from us. This heritage and legacy from Jesus Christ Himself is too rarely talked about. Instead of savoring such a gift, we concentrate on the dark night of the soul and the pain and anxiety that the silence of God may bring to us. We certainly encounter these real hurdles in our journey toward God, as we face cruel disappointments, fears, frustrations, puzzling uncertainties, and even harrowing moments when it seems that God has deserted us and our poverty is overwhelming.

As priests, we are men of God; and as men of God, we are men of hope. We must be cautious about placing our sense of hope, or the lack thereof, in either the successes or failures we experience, of which we will have both. As Mother Teresa said, God does not ask for success, only fidelity. And fidelity in the face of crushing failure is a quality dear to the heart of Christ. As Christ's men, we should expect to come face-to-face with our limitations because we do not depend upon ourselves but rather upon His saving help and His healing grace. I repeat what I said previously: *"The only real problem we have is discouragement ... and there is never a reason for discouragement."*

The priest who wrote those words, St. Peter Canisius, founded at least a dozen colleges, contributed significantly to the re-evangelized Europe after the Reformation, wrote prodigiously (giving us the first Catechism), translated the writings of the Fathers of the Church, and laid the groundwork for the Catholic Reformation north of the Alps. In the midst of his labors of over fifty years, he edited and published editions of the Fathers of the Church, wrote catechisms, spiritual manuals, textbooks, and over fourteen hundred letters. He founded seminaries and left behind a flourishing Catholicism wherever he went.

Yet discouragement dogged his path every step of the way. Discouragement seems to be the frequent problem of everyone who works for God. This profound truth is explained by the quote: "We believe ... in all things, visible and *invisible.*" The silence and the apparent absence of God can be a harrowing experience and has often crushed the strongest spirits. St. John Bosco, after he was fired by the aristocratic lady who wanted him to act as chaplain for her girls' school, chose to remain with the boys whom he was helping in the streets. Standing at the edge of a field, with no money or support of any kind, he cried out in agony to the Lord: "Help me!" Father Flanagan of Boys Town experienced similar sufferings. For example, in the 1930s, a cartoon appeared in the *Omaha World-Herald* depicting the entrance to Boys Town with a chain and padlock. Father Flanagan was going bankrupt, and he seemed to have exhausted all of his resources for help.

The most vivid image of this kind of discouragement that I have encountered is that of St. Peter Claver, a priest like us. Standing on the docks of Cartagena, Colombia, the slave ships docked, carrying hundreds of sick and dirty Africans bound with chains. Barely tolerated by the slave owners who crowded the docks, St. Peter Claver served the physical and spiritual needs of the slaves. Totally ignorant of the slaves' languages, St. Peter Claver worked tirelessly amidst opposition—even from most of the other priests in the city. No one who truly seeks God is spared discouragement, bringing even the strongest to tears and sometimes paralyzing the works of the most dedicated. For us, discouragement seems to come from three sources. First, from the moral struggle that every man has to face in half-defeats and half-victories which are part of the struggle and the uncertainty, at times, of how we stand before God. Second, from a loss of vision when the eyes of faith are blurred and the lights go out and all seems dark. Third, from trying to solve practical problems with spiritual tools, expecting prayer to be a substitute for decision, effort, and hard work, rather than the compass *within* these qualities. When this kind of discouragement sets in, the lifeblood of the spirit is drained away and everything seems profitless, useless, and meaningless. Sometimes, the silence of God seems impenetrable, and we just need to wait until the storm is over, with a clear understanding that God does not ask for success, recognition, or the praise of others but only for fidelity.

I remember coming across a letter by a very discouraged priest who could not understand why everything to which he put his hand seemed to turn to ashes. He wrote to a colleague of his who had shared the same disappointment:

> *Everyone who has ever labored for God or sought Him seriously has had his bleak and black moments, when all things seemed impossible and when the whole business of seeking God seemed to make no sense at all.*
>
> *As I look over the history of holiness, no one has been spared them. But I would not trade the risk and the uncertainty and the inscrutable darkness for any other way of life. There is little risk in seeking God and, as St. Teresa of Avila said long ago, "There is danger in everything."*

*That does not push back the darkness and it certainly does not make the pathway any less bleak. But at least it is good to know that we are in good company, and that others have trodden the same pathway, others who after all the bleak and black pathways were able to put "saint" before their name.*

Every bishop likely racks his brain to further the work of the Church in his diocese, and many of his projects and plans fail for lack of money, lack of competent people to carry them out, or simply, lack of time. We all tend to overload the circuit at times and to pull back on truly worthwhile projects. Eventually, we have to face failure, which can drain our spirits and trigger bleak thoughts. Some are even destroyed by God's apparent silence. Unable to endure the darkness and the silence, they wither away in fear and panic and become disillusioned. Their prayers seem to strike against a leaden heaven, and in the deepest part of their souls, they feel that God has deserted them. His promises seem to have turned to dust in the practical business of living, and His words do not seem able to reach them effectively.

In the year 1860, John Henry Newman was convinced that he was a failure. Everything to which he had put his hand as a Catholic had failed, and failed miserably. After his notorious conversion fifteen years before, he was forgotten, and every priestly work in which he thought he saw God's guiding hand was fruitless. In a remarkable book about Cardinal Newman, Archbishop Jean Honoré wrote this of him:

Withdrawn into himself, Newman felt the weight of total abandonment by his fellow-men. Such rejection, which would normally lead to despair and dejection, brought forth in Newman a spiritual lucidity that enabled him to detect a loving Providence in all his trials. He learned to accept them faithfully in a spirit of loving submission to God.... Failure constitutes the test of spiritual sincerity. It can never be desired for itself. Because it is the test of truth, it forces the conscience to break away from all illusions and false securities and recognize itself in its most authentic authenticity.[1]

Powerful advice! In particular, young priests will find it difficult to face the obstacles and difficulties that are a necessary and natural part of the work of the priesthood. They will run into setbacks, oppositions, and uncertainties that will almost make them cry out in the face of the seeming silence of God, what seems to be His massive indifference. And they will ask themselves, "Why? Why does He seem to desert those who want to serve Him most, and why does He, at times, seem to ignore the very ones who seek to serve Him faithfully? Why does He seem to leave helpless and hopeless the very ones who lean most heavily on His help and His providence?"

Though no easy answer exists as to "why" these things happen, perhaps one possibility is that we often mistake laziness for hope or idleness for prayer. Neither prayer nor hope produces passive men but, on the contrary, stirs a man to his mightiest efforts. Energy, enthusiasm, and boldness arise from the sanctuary of prayer; from hope in God comes strength that refuses to be discouraged by anything. That is, however, precisely the point of the agony of failure; for discouragement sets in when prayer and hope seem useless, and the spirit is robbed of joy, strength, and energy.

Joy is the first mark of the Holy Spirit—joy and the peace that surpasses all understanding (Cf. Phil. 4:7). St. Thomas Aquinas's surprising remedy for sadness is sleep, a nice warm bath, and conversation with friends—a rare piece of psychology that indicates something of his human wisdom. Our joy is based on something more than temperament or natural disposition. It is based squarely on *what* and in *whom* we believe. Unfortunately, when the practical affairs of their work begin to occupy and fill the horizon of genuinely spiritual priests, the great realities and truths that drew them to the priesthood fade in the face of the critical problems they encounter. As compromise after compromise set in, they become as secular as the world around them. Their spoken excuse: "You can't solve problems with Hail Mary's."

So where does our joy come from? From the success of our labors and projects? We are often unsuccessful. From the approval and recognition of our superiors? We should not count on that: they are busy with their own problems, far more varied and critical than our own. From a record of outstanding accomplishments that makes our curriculum vitae look like that of a nuclear physicist in *Who's Who*? Two days after we die, that will be forgotten, and we will be just a name in the necrology of the diocese. Our joy must be in God, in a living faith, in divine providence that never deserts us, and in a passion for something beyond the events and circumstances in which we live.

The television drama *A.D.*, a sequel to Franco Zeffirelli's *Jesus of Nazareth*, depicted the Emmaus scene. After the crucifixion, the two disciples are leaving the city, their spirits and hopes devastated and destroyed by the tragedy of the crucifixion. They meet a stranger on the road who opens their minds to the meaning of the Scriptures, and, after coming to an inn, they tell the stranger of the tragic things that have happened.

"We had hoped that it was He who would save Israel," they told Him. "But they crucified Him, hanged Him on a tree ... and now ... it's all over."

"All over?" the stranger asks solemnly. Then taking bread in His hands and breaking it in two, He hands them the pieces, the palms of His hands upturned ... and they see the mark of the nails. "All over?" He seems to say, "It is only just beginning."

When the darkness is all around us, when everything seems hopeless or useless and our own life seems to be without meaning or purpose, we must ask ourselves, "What exactly do I believe?" We believe that Jesus Christ is the Word made flesh, and we, His priests, are the extensions of Jesus Christ in our own time. This supreme reality is the firm foundation upon which we build.

Tempests will always rage; the Church has never been free of them. Two hundred years ago the whole of Europe was devastated by the French Revolution: priests were killed; bishops were murdered; religious orders were suppressed. In the midst of such turmoil, God raised up a whole army of saints in the next century. New religious orders were founded in the aftermath, and giants like Cardinal John Henry Newman rose up to defend the faith.

Today, the Church is lashed with new tempests, not the first in its history but still demoralizing—the sex scandal with priests, the shortage of vocations, dioceses filing bankruptcy, pastors stealing church funds. The mystery of the Incarnation proclaims God's interest in the whole human race and in each one of us. It is never *all over*. His wounded hands are always upturned to remind us of the price paid for our salvation.

When Pope John XXIII was asked what the Church needed at that moment in history, he answered: "What the Church needs right now is a little bit of holy madness!" St. Vincent Pallotti exhibited this holy madness. Pallotti was born in Rome in 1795, just as the French Revolution ended. Ordained a priest at the age of twenty-three, he was a Doctor of Theology. He initially taught at the Sapienza University in Rome but resigned the position to evangelize Rome. Imagine! Evangelize Rome! Father Pallotti was a veritable dynamo. He organized schools for shoemakers, tailors, coachmen, carpenters, gardeners, and workers of all kinds. He set up evening classes for farmers and unskilled workers who needed jobs. He gave his books, his possessions, and even his clothes to the poor. Father Pallotti founded two religious orders, established a missionary order in England, and set up several colleges for the training of priests—and he died at the age of fifty-five. The life and work of Father Pallotti exemplifies the "holy madness" Pope John XXIII was talking about, and he canonized Father Pallotti in 1962, the year the Second Vatican Council opened.

Teaching us another lesson about our priesthood, the powerful novel by Graham Greene, *The Power and the Glory*, depicts the life of a priest in Mexico during the persecutions of the Church in the 1920s. He was everything a that priest should not be: a drunken womanizer who had a child by a woman with whom he lived—someone who betrayed his priesthood in every possible way. And everybody knew it. He was a coward and hid in a province of Mexico where he was safe from the persecutions. Lured out of his hiding place to give the sacraments to a dying man, he was arrested by the enemies of the Church and condemned to be executed by a firing squad. In his jail cell, he converses with the military officer who will see to his execution the next morning. The priest explains to the officer, who despises everything the priest is and stands for, "You are a good man, and as long as you have good men, your cause will succeed. But you can't beat us; you can't win, and you can't stop us because God does not always need the best to do His work. In a pinch, he can use an old reprobate like me." God uses us, sometimes in spite of ourselves. We are weak and frail and fragile instruments, but His power works through us, often in miraculous ways.

When Catherine de Hueck, the founder of Madonna House in Canada, set up her Friendship Houses in New York to care for the poor, she came across a whole street in Brooklyn filled with Communists that were fiercely anti-Catholic. Speaking to a Jesuit friend from Fordham University, she asked him to walk down that street once a week, simply walk down the street. (The Jesuit was wearing clerical attire.) He agreed, and within two years, everyone on that street was Catholic: the power of the priesthood. If your work fails, do not be discouraged, for you bear the mystery of Christ—the One who died and brought all things to new life.

# Notes

1    Jean Honoré, *The Spiritual Journey of John Henry Newman* (New York: Alba House), 187.

# Works Cited

Brodrick, SJ, James. *Peter Canisius, 1521-97* (Baltimore: Carroll Press, 1950).

Greene, Graham. *The Power and the Glory* (New York: The Viking Press, 1946).

Honoré, Jean. *The Spiritual Journey of John Henry Newman* (New York: Alba House, 1992).

Newman, John Henry. *The Dream of Gerontius* (New York: John Lane Company, 1916).

# Priestly Holiness

S aints come in all sizes, as different from each other as apples and oranges, yet each one reflects something of Jesus Christ, some facet of His teaching or His Person. Some saints are serious and others are funny. We have tall saints and short saints, peace-loving saints and saints who fight wars, men, women, and child saints, and those who seem so far above us that we might despair of holiness for ourselves.

Priests come in all sizes also, and examining the priesthood does not mean that we are trying to fit priests into one, unbreakable mold. Rather, we want to take a good look at those qualities that give rise to an *epic priesthood*, qualities of mind and heart found in the lives of great priests, who changed the world in which they lived, who created great works for the Church and for civilization. We, encouraged by their example, must make our mark on the centuries, enlivening the Gospel in our own unique way. Pope John Paul II's exhortation in his great Apostolic Letter *Novo Millenio Ineunte* speaks to our priestly call, in words addressed directly to us:

> Now is the time for each local Church to assess its fervor and find fresh enthusiasm for its spiritual and pastoral responsibilities, by reflecting on what the Spirit of God has been saying to the People of God in this special year of grace ... so that the Church may shine

ever more brightly in the variety of her gifts
and in unity, as she journeys on (*NMI* 3).

The pastoral blueprint proposed by John Paul II was
to enter into the mind and heart of Jesus Christ, to bow in
awe before the mystery of His coming, and from that, to
draw the "particular form that fits ... the actual situation of
each local Church" (*NMI* 3). He visualized a pastoral pragmatic with a detailed understanding of local needs. The Pope
outlined the true pastoral pragmatic in the practical business
of running a parish: we must remain conscious of the risen
Christ's presence among us. We cannot get lost in the crowd,
as if we were hirelings. He is beside us, with us, above us, and
below us, every step of the way. Whether we have the most
isolated and obscure parish in the diocese or the rector of
a great Cathedral, we are not alone, and we must return to
that truth again and again.

Pope John Paul II spoke of a "trusting optimism," explaining it as the very foundation of his own optimism:

> We put the question with trusting optimism,
> but without underestimating the problems
> we face. We are certainly not seduced by the
> naive expectation that, faced with the great
> challenges of our time, we shall find some
> magic formula. No, we shall not be saved by
> a formula but by a Person, and the assurance
> which he gives us: *I am with you!* (*NMI* 29).

The enduring Presence of Christ is the pastoral pragmatic,
the guiding principle, the supernatural prudence that has
guided every priest who has ever accomplished anything for

Christ and for the Church, and it enabled them to accomplish wonders. "Faith and boldness," seems to be the motto of these priests, some of them saints, who dispelled the darkness of their times and found new ways to bring the Gospel to the nations. "We are greatly helped," Pope John Paul II said, "not only by theological reflection, but also by that great heritage which is the 'lived theology of the saints.' The saints offer us precious insights which enable us to understand more easily the intuition of faith, thanks to the special enlightenment some of them have received from the Holy Spirit" (*NMI* 27).

One such saint is St. Stephen of Perm. He brought the faith to the Zyrian people beyond the Volga River in Russia, southwest of the Ural Mountains. Antedating some of the insights of the Second Vatican Council, he overcame many challenges in a remarkable way. St. Stephen was a monk of Rostov, at a time when Russian monks became missionaries in the tradition of our own St. Boniface. He believed that every people should worship God in their own language. The Zyrians, however, had no written language. To transcend this difficulty when translating the Scriptures and the liturgy into the language of the people, St. Stephen invented a new written language, based on the symbols and signs used by the Zyrians in their embroidery and skilled carvings. At first, St. Stephen did not go out preaching missions. Instead, he attracted the people to the faith by the beauty and solemnity of public worship, and he used all the arts to make worship truly impressive. Entering their Churches, the Zyrian people felt that they were truly welcomed into the House of God and participating in heavenly liturgies.

St. Stephen was a champion of the poor and oppressed, as many great bishops have been, and he became a true father in Christ to these converted people. Born among the Zyrians, he had a special love for them, and he brought them, not only the bare bones of the Christian faith, but the riches of a Christian faith and culture. He realized that evangelizing required a *culture* in which the realities of the faith make sense, and that evangelizing builds upon education, economic stability, and the arts. In addition to the Zyrian people, St. Stephen made himself thoroughly familiar with the culture and traditions of other people on the edge of civilization: Chuvashes, Mordvins, Permiaks, and Lapps. Becoming their monk-missionary in 1370, he was appointed their bishop in 1383, and he died in Moscow in 1396.

As one of the Russian saints, St. Stephen of Perm is recognized by the Catholic Church along with St. Seraphim of Sarov and St. Vladimir of Kiev. The old ways in which St. Stephen had been trained simply did not work, and he discovered new ways to spread the good news of Jesus Christ. The emphasis on the Incarnation and the conviction that he was a living instrument of Jesus Christ gave him his missionary and evangelizing method. He is a powerful example of how to create the future for Christ.

As priests of the third millennium, we should look at the landscape of our own world in the light of Pope John Paul II's words. A far different world from that which opened the twentieth century, we may find ourselves puzzled as to how we can bring our world to Christ and Christ to our world. We may have to fashion new tools and new instruments to further the mission of Christ in a world that opposes every truth and value we cherish. So where do we start? What is the primary prudential judgment we are to make, even before we put our hands to the task?

In a sermon preached at St. Mary's at Oxford on January 22, 1832, John Henry Newman asked why the apostles had succeeded in their work, in spite of the massive obstacles to the mission entrusted to them:

> Whence, then, was it that in spite of all these impediments to their success, they succeeded? How did they gain that place in the world which they hold to this day, enabling them to perpetuate principles distasteful to the majority of those who profess to receive them? What is the hidden attribute of the Truth, and how does it act, prevailing, as it does, single-handedly, over the many and multiform errors, by which it is simultaneously and incessantly attacked?[1]

Newman's answer: *personal influence*. By that, he meant the character and conviction of those who spread the Gospel in that pagan world. Their own personal witness to what they believed and its embodiment in their total personalities convinced others.

One of the saddest, yet most insightful, passages in the Gospels is: "The children of this world are more prudent in dealing with their own generation than are the children of light" (Lk. 16:8). In other words, those who labor for this earthly city maximize human genius and initiative (e.g., computer geniuses, master-planners of cities, pioneers in physics and medical science, superb actors). Regrettably, those who labor for the things of God are often satisfied with the mediocre, second-best.

If Pope John Paul II's appeal to evangelize the world of the twenty-first century is to be realized, the pastoral vision satisfied with mediocrity must be reversed. Though many great things are being done, they often go unnoticed because those laboring are intent on the mission rather than recognition for its fruits. Pope John Paul II thus encouraged us:

> The program of the Gospel must continue to take root, as it has always done, in the life of the Church everywhere. It is *in the local churches* that the specific features of a detailed pastoral plan can be identified—goals and methods, formation and enrichment of the people involved, the search for necessary resources—which enable the proclamation of Christ to reach people, mold communities, and have a deep and incisive influence in bringing the Gospel values to bare upon society and culture (*NMI* 29).

In this Apostolic Letter, Pope John Paul II recalled the great events and graces of the Jubilee Year: purification of memory, asking forgiveness for the pilgrim Church's failures of the past, canonizations, the army of pilgrims who participated in the festivities in Rome, the young people who delighted the Pope's heart by their presence, the International Eucharistic Congress, the Pope's own pilgrimage to Mount Sinai and the Holy Land, and reaching out to other Christians—especially Christians of the East. "Starting afresh from Christ," Pope John Paul II emphasized, "the

Jubilee Year must be translated into pastoral initiatives" that will bring the Catholic heritage alive at every level, reaching the depths of the human person and transforming lives, parishes, and communities with the vision that flows from this Jubilee of the Incarnation (*NMI* 29).

The first thing to communicate to our people is the dimensions of holiness that the Catholic faith holds out to them. Holiness is not the prerogative of priests and religious. Rather, as the Council proclaimed, the universal call to holiness is sealed in the soul of every baptized person. Holiness, the Holy Father warned us,

> ... must not be misunderstood as if it involved some extraordinary existence, possible only for a few "uncommon heroes" of holiness. The ways of holiness are many, according to the vocation of each individual. I thank the Lord that in these years he has enabled me to beatify and canonize a large number of Christians, and among them many lay people who attained holiness in the most ordinary circumstances of life ... It would be a contradiction to settle for a life of mediocrity, marked by a minimal ethic and a shallow religiosity" (*NMI* 31).

It might seem surprising that the first priority Pope John Paul II identified for pastoral planning was a program of holiness, but holiness is the whole purpose of the Gospel and evangelization. Without holiness, we cannot please God. Without the flame of holiness burning in our hearts, we are nothing but "resounding gong[s]" and "clashing cymbal[s]" (1 Cor. 13:2): just a lot of noise and clatter.

Almost a hundred years ago, Cistercian Dom Jean Baptiste Chautard wrote a book titled *The Soul of the Apostolate*; it was the favorite bedside book of Pope St. Pius X. The book is precisely about holiness and insists that we, priests in particular, who are on the front lines of spreading the Gospel, must not settle for a life of mere activity. The book is a powerful plea for holiness—the fruit of authentic interiority—as the first effort in priestly life. This call to holiness was also the message of Pope John Paul II to us: *Look to your own soul first!*

Pope John Paul II was well aware of this message throughout the history of the Church. About 850 years ago, Eugenius III, a monk of the monastery of Clairvaux in France where St. Bernard was the founder and abbot, was elected pope. Bernard, fearing that the new Pope would get too involved in the business of running the Church and preoccupied with mere administrative duties, wrote a book for Eugenius called *De Consideratione*, which can be loosely translated "On Looking Into Yourself." In the book, he gave the Pope what might appear as very strange advice: "Don't let those damnable occupations keep you from taking care of the soul of your mother's only son." What occupations did he call *damnable*? Why, Eugenius's responsibilities as Pope: the running of the Church. Those responsibilities would be *damnable* if they occupied the Pope at the cost of his own spiritual life, his own pursuit of holiness, his own intimacy with God.

The great saint of this same message is St. Francis de Sales, who wrote his classic work, *Introduction to a Devout Life*, for a married woman. At that time, it was thought that only priests, monks, and religious could be holy; but St. Francis, a bishop and a spiritual director, disagreed, and had this startling thing to say: "It is not only erroneous, but a heresy, to hold that life in the army, the workshop, the court or the home is incompatible with holiness." Some people so disagreed with his teaching that his book was burned from several pulpits.

The paths to holiness are manifold, and no two people follow exactly the same pathway. The great army of saints in the Church bears witness to this truth. Pope John Paul II said that the call to Baptism itself, the incorporation of the Christian into Christ, is the call to holiness. The call to holiness is primary, but for each one of us, the pathway is unique, since our holiness blossoms from the soil of our own particular existence.

At the same time, we must insist that *nothing in human life is outside the scope of holiness*. Everything that is not sinful can be integrated into our relationship with God, can become the fuel of holiness. St. Thomas Aquinas, one of the great masters of holiness, was aware of this truth when he wrote, "Contemplation is good for the soul ... but so is a good warm bath!" We must insist that holiness, and this is the heart of Pope John Paul II's words, is in everything. All aspects of human life, except sin, can be integrated into a saint's life with God. There is a holy way to pray and to sing and to dance; there is a holy way to work and to drink beer and to fly kites; there is a holy way to play tennis and to marry and to wash dishes. The scope of holiness is as broad as human life itself, and any action not sinful in itself can be made part of our search for God.

We must not separate the pursuit of holiness from our own particular life, obligations, duties, and wholesome activities. The challenge and unique opportunity is for us to make the whole of our lives a hymn of praise to God. Our efforts should be focused on integrating every aspect of our life into a living and dynamic relationship with God. Pope John Paul II offers the source of this integration:

This training in holiness calls for a Christian life distinguished above all in *the art of prayer*.... Prayer develops that conversation with Christ which makes us His intimate friends: "Abide in me and I in you" (Jn 15:4). This reciprocity is the very substance and soul of the Christian life, and the condition of all true pastoral life.

> [O]ur Christian communities must become *genuine "schools" of prayer*, where the meeting with Christ is expressed not just in imploring help but also in thanksgiving, praise, adoration, contemplation, listening and ardent devotion, until the heart truly "falls in love." Intense prayer, yes, but it does not distract us from our commitment to history: by opening our heart to the love of God it also opens it to the love of our brothers and sisters, and makes us capable of shaping history according to God's plan (*NMI* 32, 33).

Prayer is the deliberate and conscious turning to God in all the events and problems of life, and the habit of prayer blossoms into a constant and continual hope in God. Those who are doing the work of Christ must be in continual contact and conversation with Him through prayer, which brings alive every human possibility and every personal responsibility. Prayer does not make men and women passive. Rather it keeps alive that consciousness of God, who should be the intimate companion of all that we do.

Prayer is often difficult because insensitivity to God has become an entrenched attitude. Genuine prayer, because it is true communion with God, keeps expectations high. It prevents that lowering of expectations that often comes with "experience" and that loss of idealism that some look upon as maturity. True prayer nourishes a genuine idealism and does not permit ideals to die in the arena of practical affairs. True prayer, flowing from our union with Christ within the concrete circumstances of our own life, bears spiritual fruit. Pastoral fruitfulness is based upon the ability of the priest to lean upon the fidelity of God and to educate himself in the true dimensions of hope.

Prayer is more like a culture, an atmosphere, an environment in which we live, than a passing act or event, and it leads to the deepest affirmation about who we are and about God's intentions for us. Prayer speaks not only out of the depths of our own soul but also as part of a living tradition, the religious heritage in which we participate. And, as Pope John Paul II reminded us, our heritage of prayer is very rich.

> The great mystical tradition of the Church of both East and West has much to say in this regard. It shows how prayer can progress, as a genuine dialogue of love, to the point of rendering the person wholly possessed by the divine Beloved.... This is the lived experience of Christ's promise: "He who loves me will be loved by My Father, and I will love him and manifest myself to him" (Jn. 14:21)....

It would be wrong to think that ordinary Christians can be content with a shallow prayer that is unable to fill their whole life (*NMI* 33, 34).

Prayer expresses and defines the kind of person we are. Prayer nourishes and develops a definite and specific personality, with the full burden of human qualities and the historical circumstances of an individual life. It must eventually touch every aspect of our lives, laying our whole existence open to the naked gaze of God. I am a definite person, with a past, a history, a blend of qualities and characteristics quite unlike any other. No one has ever walked my particular path. No other person has been shaped by the forces that shaped my life. My prayer must express and define the particular person that I am and every aspect of my particular life.

Pope John Paul II asked for this totality of prayer, and he was convinced that every Catholic, whatever his vocation and walk of life, could enter into this life of prayer. Pope John Paul II considered the prayer of all the faithful so fundamental that he issued this directive: "It is therefore essential that *education in prayer* should become in some way the key-point of all pastoral planning" (*NMI* 34). Pope John Paul II was encouraging and inculcating a prudence that belongs uniquely to the priestly vocation, a pastoral and practical prudence, aimed at more than the mere managing of resources or the planning of parish and liturgical events. Like the chief shepherd that he was, Pope John Paul II demonstrated how to be the Good Shepherds of our flocks, as we form both them and ourselves to the image of Christ.

Priestly holiness is *our* kind of justice: what we owe to God, to the Church, to our people, and to the world. Without holiness, we are merely administrators of Church temporalities and parishes, centers of capital management. Without holiness, we are professionals among professionals, with God reduced to a concept or exiled to the periphery of our existence. We can forget that the very nature of priesthood is immersion in the mystery of God, a mystery that must shine in our eyes and exude from every pore of our bodies.

You and I, looking out over the Church in the midst of the scandals that have shaken the Catholic priesthood at this time in history, must desire, in the deepest parts of our souls, to make up in our own lives for the disgrace that has stained this holiest of vocations. It reminds me of St. Aloysius Gonzaga, that shining young prince of the Gonzagas, living in the midst of a corrupt Renaissance court and, after a fierce battle with his father, winning the freedom to consecrate himself to God. Looking over the state of the priesthood and religious life in Renaissance Italy, St. Aloysius asked himself the question, "Who will make up to the Lord for this betrayal on every side?" With no hint of self-conceit or a holier-than-thou attitude, he answered, "I will."

Aloysius, however, was not the plaster-cast saint that so many images of him seem to indicate. He fought heroically to free himself from the moral corruption of Renaissance court life, but he was fully aware of the tainted stock from which he had sprung. When other Jesuit novices and even some of the mature Jesuits started to treat him as if he had been a saint from the day of his birth, he reminded them,

"Did you know that I learned to swear when I was five years old?" At the age of five, the favorite of the rough soldiers in his father's castle, Aloysius picked up the language of these military men and scandalized everyone by throwing words around that would have shocked a sailor. He was told firmly but clearly by his tutor that gentlemen did not use that kind of language, and only later did he realize what the words meant. But he would use the childhood story to dispel the idea that there are any ready-made saints.

To say that Aloysius was fully aware of his faults, weaknesses, and defects of character does not diminish St. Aloysius's shining sanctity. He found himself irritated with his own faults and realized that we are all plagued by elements of self-ignorance and self-esteem and that we can become angry with ourselves for faults and failures that reveal the hidden roots of our motivation. When dealing with his faults, Aloysius simply said, "See, Lord, the fruits of my garden," expressed his sorrow, and moved on. And when he noticed something outside his control, he simply disregarded it. He never tried for the impossible. Such balance makes St. Aloysius such an extraordinary example for priests.

The only answer to the renewal of the priesthood is the determination of each priest to pledge, in the secret of his soul, to be truly holy, to become a saint. Can we really aim for anything less? Whenever the Church or the world has been in crisis, God always raises up saints.

In this business of holiness, we are wise to look carefully into what constitutes genuine holiness. Many of the older spiritual books hold out almost impossible ideals, sometimes rather inhuman, and all that we can do in the face of such exhortations to holiness is shrug our shoulders and say, "Well, that's not for me." The only reaction to an impossible ideal is to give up and let mediocrity set in. But holiness, and holiness alone, will bring us out of the present crisis in the priesthood. It must grow from the soil of our own life and existence. Holiness is concrete, unique in every person; and in the whole calendar of the saints, no two are exactly alike.

St. Bernard of Clairvaux, a stunning preacher, was tempted to think that he was really good at preaching. The thought came in the midst of a truly great sermon. At first, he was shocked by the thought, but he then told the devil that he did not begin the sermon for *him* and that he would not stop for *him*. Many of us have a remarkable set of talents. Most of us are bright, well-educated, often highly-esteemed by others, and often in the spotlight. Some of us even become famous, see our names in print, and are told how well we are liked and how we brighten up a room when we walk into it. We certainly should take all this in stride because it usually means that we are reflecting someone greater than ourselves. We should not be afraid to embrace the fact that we do reflect that *Someone*, the mystery of His indwelling presence. Holiness simply means that we enter deeper and deeper into that mysterious presence which becomes the very center of our existence. Holiness is not for someone else. Holiness is for all of us.

We never know what priestly ministry is going to demand of us. We are creatures of obedience and are often asked by our bishops to tackle almost impossible tasks. In some cases, those tasks are outside the parish ministry, some kind of specialized work or ministry. We may be called upon to reach and serve people outside the borders of a parish, a school, or even our diocese. This is when priestly holiness and dedication have to show themselves to the world. The face we show the world, alien and different as it may be, may make the difference between showing Christ's face to the world and allowing it to remain hidden for all kinds of reasons.

Consider the example of Father Jerzy Popieluszko. When Pope John Paul II returned to Poland in June of 1979, his visit, in spite of its obvious spiritual import, carried with it criticism of the communist regime. Pope John Paul II words were bold and explicit: "Do not be afraid to insist on your rights. Refuse a life based on lies and double thinking. Do not be afraid to suffer for Christ." Father Jerzy Popieluszko, a young priest living in Warsaw and working as a chaplain to university students, took these words seriously. But he found himself assigned to another ministry: chaplain to the Solidarity movement. When the Gdańsk ship workers went on strike in August 1980, steelworkers in Warsaw joined them in solidarity. They sent a request to the chancery office of the Archdiocese for a priest to come and celebrate Mass. Father Popieluszko was given the assignment. The Mass in front of the factory was an extraordinary turning point in the young priest's life. He suddenly realized that the workers' struggle for justice and freedom was a spiritual struggle; and so, with his Bishop's consent, he became chaplain to the striking workers.

In December of 1981, the government declared martial law and thousands of Solidarity members and their supporters were arrested. Thus, Father Jerzy's pastoral duties included visiting the prisoners and organizing support for their families. At the same time, through his "patriotic sermons," he, like John Paul II, emphasized the moral and spiritual dimensions of the Solidarity cause. The government claimed that this was no business of the Church, but Father Jerzy said openly:

> It is not only the hierarchy but the millions of believers who in the broadest sense embody the Church. So when people suffer and are persecuted, the Church feels the pain. The mission of the Church is to be with the people and to share their joys and sorrows. My vocation as a priest is to serve God by seeking a way to human hearts. To serve God is to speak about evil as a sickness which should be brought to light so that it can be cured. To serve God is to condemn evil in all its manifestations.[2]

As his popularity grew, the government looked for ways to silence Father Jerzy. He was subjected to numerous forms of petty harassment and was followed everywhere he went. His Masses were very often interrupted by yelling and screaming. A bomb was hurled against his apartment. His remarks about this incident were quoted everywhere: "The only thing we should fear is the betrayal of Christ for a few silver pieces of meaningless peace."

Father Jerzy's kindness, even to those who persecuted him, was legendary. At Christmas, he visited communist soldiers on duty, bringing them small gifts and refreshments. He refused to give up, and he also refused to hate. He was arrested and indicted, but the outcry from the workers was so great that he was released. Someone suggested to his bishop that he be sent away to study, for his own safety, but the priest refused to go.

On the night of October 19, 1984, Father Jerzy was abducted by three men who stuffed him in the trunk of a car and drove off. His driver managed to escape and reported what had happened. Masses were said throughout the country for his safe return. Later, four members of the security police confessed that, after savagely beating Father Jerzy, they had tied him up, weighted his body with stones, and tossed him, still alive, into a reservoir.

Father Jerzy's example of priestly courage and holiness reverberated through Poland. Five years later, in the first free elections in postwar Poland, the people overthrew the communist government and elected a Solidarity government. The power of priestly holiness is not confined to the parish or the school. Sometimes it impacts the whole destiny of a nation.

# Notes

1    John Henry Newman, *Personal Influence: the Means of Propagating the Truth*, University Sermons, Sermon V.
2    Robert Ellsberg, *All Saints* (New York: Crossroad Publishing Company, 1999) 456-458.

# Works Cited

Chautard, O.C.S.O., Dom Jean Baptiste. *The Soul of the Apostolate* (Trappist, KY: Abbey of Gethsemani, 1945).

Ellsberg, Robert. *All Saints* (New York: Crossroad Publishing Company, 1999).

Martindale, C.C. *The Vocation of St. Aloysius Gonzaga* (New York: S.J. Sheed & Ward, 1945).

McGinley, Phyllis. *Saint-Watching* (New York: The Viking Press, 1969).

Newman, John Henry. *Personal Influence: the Means of Propagating the Truth*, University Sermons, Sermon V.

Pope John Paul II, *Novo Millenio Ineunte*, 2001.

Potok, Chaim. *The Chosen* (New York: Ballantine Books, 1967).

Sheed, F.J., *ed. Saints Are Not Sad* (New York: Sheed & Ward, 1949).

St. Bernard of Clairvaux, *De Consideratione*, II.2.

St. Francis de Sales, *Introduction to a Devout Life* (New York: Image Books, Doubleday, 1993).

St. Thomas Aquinas, *Disputed Questions de Veritate* trans. Robert Mulligan,

S.J., James V. McGlynn, S.J., and Robert W. Schmidt, S.J. (Chicago: Henry Regnery Company, 1952).

Stevens, Reverend Clifford. *The One Year Book of Saints* (Huntington: Our Sunday Visitor Press, 1989).

Thurston, Herbert and Donald Atwater, *eds. Butler's Lives of the Saints* (New York: P. J. Kenedy and Sons, 1962).

# The Courageous and Steadfast Man

aia Wojciechowska is a native of Poland who came to the United States as the Nazis invaded Poland in 1939. Her father had been the head of the Polish Air Force and had fled the country with his family. English was not Wojciechowska's native language, but she mastered it, graduated from Immaculate Heart College in Los Angeles, and worked for a time during World War II for Radio Free Europe, beaming broadcasts in Polish to her home country. Wojciechowska also became a writer of books for young people, writing stories with morals about courage and honesty and sheer goodness. One of those stories was "Shadow of a Bull." The story is of Manolo, the son of a famous matador in Spain. His father died from a bullfighting injury, and everyone expects Manolo to follow in the footsteps of his father. But Manolo does not want to be a matador. He wants to be a doctor. His test of courage comes when he has to tell the people of his village that he is not going to follow in the footsteps of his father, that he wants to do something else.

Courage comes in many forms, and not only the great and obvious heroes need courage. Manolo's neighbors thought his courage would be shown in the bullring, facing the bull, waving a cloak, and brandishing a sword. But his courage was to go against public opinion and to choose his own destiny by becoming a doctor. Courage is part of all of our lives, but we all experience it in different ways. For some, courage is speaking out at the right time; for others, courage is keeping silent rather than speaking. For some, it is doing things quietly and without notice; for others, it is doing something that others are sure to see. For some, it is showing kindness; for others, it is accepting kindness. For some, it is patient endurance; for others, it is taking action as a matter of conscience. For some, it is overcoming fear; for others, it is overcoming foolhardiness. Whatever its form, courage is a necessary part of everyday living. No one can escape from those moments which demand a special kind of courage.

The purpose of the Gospels, Cardinal Newman wrote, is not simply to give us doctrines we should believe but to give us doctrines that will assist us in developing moral character. The development of courage is an essential part of such character. Such development comes through faith and is hastened by prayer. Prayer molds character so that we may respond properly to unplanned adversity. In such a crucible as that, true courage shows itself. We may not be called into action on the battlefield, and we may not be called to undergo great persecution or to accept martyrdom. Mostly, we need courage in everyday life so that we can face the call to do the right thing, in spite of our fears. Dorothy Bernard, an American actress from the silent movie era, once stated, "Courage is fear that has said its prayers."

Courage is not only for soldiers going into battle or for martyrs facing death. Courage is a quality of the steadfast man. We, priests, need it every day of our lives. In fact, we need supernatural courage to take on the responsibilities and obligations of the Catholic priesthood. Fortunately, that courage will doubtlessly be given to us when and where we need it; we have only to ask for it.

Father Vincent McNabb was an old English Dominican who lived in London in the first half of the twentieth century and was known for his asceticism and humor. He was a regular preacher of the Catholic Evidence Guild at Hyde Park and was a close friend of G.K. Chesterton, Hilaire Belloc, and other members of what was known as the English Catholic Renaissance. A delightful book about him was written by one of his favorite hecklers at Hyde Park, a Jewish businessman, who saw something of a rare holiness in this crotchety old Dominican.

Father McNabb had a wonderful way with children and used to say that if a person could not explain the deepest mysteries of Religion to a child, he, himself, did not understand them. He was once asked by a group of children, "Father Vincent, what would you do if the enemies of the Church took over this country and told you that you must deny your faith or be killed?" Father McNabb answered very quickly, "Oh, I'd apostatize, of course. I am a weak man; pray for me." He knew that if courage was needed, it had to be given by God so that he did not have to depend only upon his own strength.

The courage about which I am talking is the fruit of faith, the finest product of faith, the stability that comes from faith, the backbone and arm of faith. Courage is born in the white heat of battle, a battle that, perhaps, no one will ever know or hear about because it occurs within us. Such courage assures us that we will live by our conscience in every crisis we face. No doubt, these crises will not be rare or infrequent, if we are truly the men of God whom we claim to be. Courage is really the blood and guts of the priesthood, a priesthood that bids us to communion with the Blessed Trinity when we would often rather remain on the superficial level of societal custom.

One stunning example of the opposite of courage is the following story about cowardice. The story is not one of moral theology but one of flesh-and-blood reality. Moreover, the story is about a priest, a parish priest, who failed to have courage when courage was the only alternative to following his conscience. This example of cowardice is found in *The Betrothed* by Alessandro Manzoni, and is about a young couple in seventeenth century Italy who want to marry and who approach the priest in their village to make arrangements for the marriage. Unbeknownst to her, the girl in the story has caught the eye of a nobleman of the village, and he threatens the priest with death if the priest officiates at the marriage of the young couple. The whole novel is about this young couple trying to get married and the terrible problems that they encounter as they seek to become husband and wife. The priest shows himself to be a coward in the face of the threats of the nobleman who controls the village, and he neglects his God-given duty out of fear.

The story of the priest's cowardice reaches the ears of his bishop, Cardinal Federigo Borromeo, and the Cardinal visits the village to look into the matter. In a powerful scene, the Cardinal remonstrates the priest for his lack of courage and tells the priest that in the face of danger, the priest should have prayed. The priest thinks the Cardinal is unreasonable; after all, argues the priest, he was faced with *death*, and a violent death, at that. What else should he have done? "Courage," the priest says, "isn't a thing a man gives himself if he hasn't got it." The story continues:

> "Then I should ask you," the Cardinal replie[s], "why you ever took on a ministry which demands that you should struggle against the world and its passions. But I would rather ask you a different question. Since in this ministry, however you come to enter it, courage is necessary for the fulfillment of your duties, how have you failed to reflect that there is One Who will infallibly give you courage when you ask Him for it? Do you think all those millions of martyrs were courageous by nature, that they naturally held life in so little account? They all had courage because courage was necessary, and they had trust."
>
> "Knowing your weakness and your own duties, did you ever think of preparing yourself for difficult situations that might overtake you? Surely, if you loved those who have been entrusted to your spiritual care ... surely, when you saw the two of them threatened together with yourself ... you must have begged for strength to overcome all fears, to expel them as temptations? At least you must have felt that holy and noble fear *for others*.... that fear should have urged you to do everything possible to avert the danger that was threatening *them*."[1]

Courage is not simply for our own sake but for the sake of others. Very few of us find ourselves in the kind of desperate situation described in *The Betrothed*, but we face many other situations, not quite so dramatic, every day. Not one of us can escape from them. We are all tempted to be cowards in little things, even trifling things.

A bishop wears red to remind him that he should be ready, at any time, under any circumstances, to lay down his life for his flock; many have, and many do. No one is equal to that kind of sacrifice, and no one depends upon his own strength should that sacrifice be demanded. And we have no way of knowing when, or if, that will be demanded of us.

Not so long ago, on July 10, 1970, a frail and elderly man left the company of government guards and walked across the bridge linking mainland China and the island of Hong Kong. On the other side, he was embraced by a crowd of friends and fellow Maryknoll missionaries who had come to welcome him to freedom. After twelve years in prison, the last foreign missionary in communist China was on his way home.

This was Bishop James Walsh,[2] one of the first priests of the Maryknoll Mission Society, who had worked all of his priestly life in China, was named bishop in 1927, served as Superior General of Maryknoll, and afterwards, returned to Shanghai. In 1948, the Communist Revolution reached Shanghai. Bishop Walsh was harassed; his classmate, Bishop Francis Ford, died in a communist prison in 1952, and Bishop Walsh declared that he would never voluntarily leave China. Bishop Walsh explained:

At a time when the Catholic religion is being persecuted with the design of eliminating it from China, I think it is the plain duty of all Catholic missioners ... to remain where they are until prevented from doing so by physical force. If interment should intervene in the case of some, even death, I think it should simply be regarded as a normal risk that is inherent in our state of life ... as a small price to pay for carrying out our duty.

Bishop Walsh believed that the vocation of the priest is not simply represented by his occupational work—whether teaching, preaching, or performing pastoral duties. The vocation is the same, even if all these activities are stripped away. "If we start to pick and choose for ourselves, it is very hard to tell if we are carrying out our vocation or running away from it."

Bishop Walsh's convictions were soon severely tested. He was arrested in China in 1958 and charged with conspiracy and espionage. For two years, he was held in solitary confinement and subjected to endless interrogation sessions. He was then formally "convicted" and sentenced to 20 years in prison. At the age of 79, after twelve years in prison, spending most of his time praying the Rosary and studying a Chinese dictionary, he was taken to the border of China and freed. Bishop Walsh's remarks about his imprisonment reveal much about his vision of priesthood: "I was a Catholic priest, and my people were in trouble. So I simply stayed with them as all priests should do at such times."

The dangers that we, priests, face are not so blatant and not so physical. They are more subtle, bound up with the very culture in which we live, but they require just as much courage and strength of spirit. The dangers to our flocks are everywhere, and we sometimes must risk facing them squarely.

I know a priest who told his people very frankly that to sell and make available to others pornographic videos, in their stores or service stations, was sinful and a clear betrayal of the principles of their religion. The community was in an uproar. Parishioners said, "How could you dare to say such things from the pulpit and threaten the livelihood of good and well-meaning people?" The priest was adamant; the bishop supported him, and there were a few empty pews in his church on Sunday. But he was right, and it took courage for him to say what was true.

Another priest whom I know answered the rectory doorbell one afternoon and found an African-American girl asking for help. Her car had broken down just outside of town, and she needed help to continue on her way to meet her husband, who was an officer at a nearby military base. The priest invited her in, called a local service station to take care of her car, and arranged for her to stay in a local motel until the next morning. The following day, he sent her on her way with a little cash to take care of needed expenses. As one parishioner later said, "The tongues began to wag; gossip was all over town, and some people in the parish were not happy that kindness was shown to one of *those* people."

The next Sunday, the priest stood at the pulpit and told his parishioners what he thought of their Catholicism. He told them bluntly that racial prejudice of any kind was a sin and, in this case, perhaps a serious sin, and that he simply would not tolerate that kind of prejudice in his parish. It took courage for him to say those things.

Yet another priest, a dedicated and devoted pastor of a well-to-do parish, convinced his parish council that 10 percent of the parish's income should go to the support of a poorer parish in the diocese. At the end of the year, because of a change in financial circumstances, it became clear that if the wealthy parish were to fulfill its commitment to the poor parish, the wealthy parish would go into the red. But the priest of that parish insisted: "We made a commitment, and we are going to keep it, whatever the consequences."

On the parish council was a very wealthy member of the parish, a successful businessman and prominent member of the local community. As he heard the pastor speak those words, he held up his hand to speak. "Father, I am a business-man, and I know poor business methods when I see them. I give $2,500 to this parish every quarter, and if you are not going to run this parish on a sound business basis, I will not continue my support." As he said these words, he held up a check in his hand. Reaching over and taking the check from the man's hand, the priest said: "What makes you think God needs your money!" Then the priest ripped up the check. Later, the wealthy man's wife told the pastor, "No priest ever dared to speak to him that way. It's the best thing that ever happened to him."

In 1964, the American bishops told their priests to preach on social justice, race prejudice, and the evil of racial discrimination. The bishops told the priests to avoid any-thing explicitly political while stressing the moral implica-tions of policy issues for Catholics. A priest on an Air Force base gave a strong sermon on the subject, as the bishops had directed, stressing the seriousness of race prejudice and Catholic teaching on the subject, even quoting the encyclicals of Pope Pius XII and Pope John XXIII. After the Mass, a prominent colonel and a member of the parish, came back to the sacristy and berated the priest for speaking of such a matter from the pulpit.

"I had a devil of a time," the Colonel said, "getting my children into a decent school when I was stationed in Washington, D.C. because of this hullabaloo over civil rights. The Blacks are taking over everywhere, and I don't like it. I don't agree with anything you said, and I think you should keep politics out of the pulpit."

"Colonel," the priest said, "Now you know how a black man feels when he cannot get his children into a decent school and has to suffer in all kinds of ways simply because he is black. When he travels with his family, he has no idea whether he can find a decent place to put up for the night, and sometimes people won't even serve him and his family in a restaurant. You don't have to agree with anything I said in that sermon, but don't you pretend to be a Catholic."

A captain speaking that way to a colonel could have been removed from the Air Force. But the Captain was also a Catholic priest, and the Colonel was his parishioner. For the welfare of this parishioner, the Captain-priest had to receive the courage to correct an officer of higher rank. Knowing that the welfare of the Colonel standing before God was at stake, the priest chose the way of courage. We are all asked to do the same and to do such for the same reason.

My courage serves the spiritual welfare of my people. Release this courage within me, Lord.

# Notes

1    Alessandro Manzoni, *The Betrothed* (New York: Penguin Books, 1972), 474-475.
2    Robert Ellsbert, *All Saints* (New York: Crossroads Publishing Company, 1999), 190-191.

# Works Cited

Bouyer, Louis. *Newman: His Life and Spirituality* (New York: P.J. Kenedy & Sons, 1958).

Ellsbert, Robert. *All Saints* (New York: Crossroads Publishing Company, 1999).

Manzoni, Alessandro. *The Betrothed* (New York: Penguin Books,1972).

Siderman, E.A. *A Saint in Hyde Park* (Maryland: Paulist, 1950).

Wojciechowska, Maia. *Shadow of a Bull* (New York: Simon & Schuster, 1992).

# Temperance

At this moment in history, we must cultivate the conviction that striving for holiness alone will bring us through the terrible times in which we live; and we are deceiving ourselves if we do not recognize that striving for holiness is our perennial mission. But who can hope to live up to that ideal and challenge in the shifting sands upon which we live, with social bombshells and barriers facing us on every side, in a world that has become almost totally pagan in its aspirations and its vision of human worth? Holiness is our only option: without hesitation, without compromise, without anything resembling false humility or subtle forms of vanity. If we are to change the world in which we live and work, only holiness will bring about that change. There is no other option.

Holiness is built upon a life of virtue. One such virtue that creates a foundation strong enough to support the journey to holiness is temperance. The quality we call temperance has been the subject of learned treatises; its definition is usually reduced to practicing moderation in food and drink, and keeping a careful custody of the eyes and heart—making sure that our thoughts do not wander in forbidden directions. But that is not the meaning of the original concept, which is far richer and more expansive, expressed by the Greek word *sophrosyne*.

A few years ago, a priest friend of mine and a student of the Classics, was astonished to find at the Classics Department of his state university, a remarkable computer called

*Ibycus*, the result of a collaboration between the University of California, the University of Pennsylvania, Harvard University, and the son and heir of the Hewlitt family, one of the founders of Hewlitt-Packard. The three universities had fed into *Ibycus* the classic writings in Hebrew, Greek, and Latin and had created a research tool which, at the time, was truly groundbreaking. So my friend approached the Chairman of the Classics Department of the university and asked if he could access all of the passages where Aristotle uses the word *sophrosyne*. "Certainly," the Classics department Chair replied. He sat down at *Ibycus*, typed in the word, and waited for the results. In just a few minutes, the printout appeared, noting passage after passage where Aristotle had used that word in his writings. As it turns out, Aristotle gives the quality that we call *temperance* a vastly different meaning than we do.

By Aristotle's definition, *sophrosyne* is what we call *character*, a mind and a disposition that has complete control of itself because it is rooted in deeply-shaped convictions and a sensitivity of conscience that recognizes the first approach of danger. Since we face many moral dangers today, appropriating this more focused understanding of the virtue of temperance is very useful. The pull of such dangers attracts us, and those whom we call saints had to walk through the flames of passion to move from virtue to holiness.

After the death of St. Francis de Sales, when officials from Rome were considering his cause for canonization, a commission of auditors was sent from Rome to interview St. Jane Frances de Chantal on the life of her spiritual director and friend. They had a roster of virtues about which they wanted to consult her and asked frank questions about St. Francis de Sales's practice of chastity.

St. Jane Frances de Chantal's answers were just as frank. "Don't think that he was never tested," she told the auditors, "or that occasions were not offered him for letting down his guard. He was tested and tried but walked through the fire unscathed." *Temperance* in this sense was more than the guarding of the eyes or the strict control of wandering thoughts. It was custody of the self, the holding of oneself in one's own hands, by a conscious and deliberate intent.

But this virtue of temperance is not sufficient, even if it is necessary. The widespread scandal that has shaken the Church in the United States indicates that something is terribly wrong with the spiritual lives of some priests, or perhaps with the spirituality they received in their formative years. They seem never to have left a certain adolescent restlessness that led them into an existential loneliness, which is often the harrowing experience of budding adolescents. For certain teenagers, adolescence is a bewildering desert where they experiment with drugs, sex, and aberrant behavior, trying to forge for themselves some kind of fragile identity, in an attempt to survive the harrowing loneliness. Since, at their age, no strong habits of goodness have been formed, adolescents often have to be rescued by concerned parents or the law. Likewise, perhaps a sound spirituality may have rescued those wayward priests from what was, perhaps, an extended adolescence.

To understand the behavior of some wayward priests, it may be helpful to look at the three traditional theological sciences that deal with human behavior, each with a different focus and goal. The three sciences are: moral theology, ascetical theology, and spiritual theology. *Moral* theology looks at human behavior in the mode of *act*, to the simple goodness or malevolence of a human act. Further, moral theology looks to the formation of *conscience*. Consciences have to be informed and formed by the truth of who we are as men and as Catholics. Our goal as morally formed men is to execute actions that are in keeping with sound moral principles and the law of God. The study of moral theology is a necessary and indispensable science for the priest in his dignity as a confessor.

*Ascetical* theology looks to human acts in the mode of *virtue*, insofar as these good human acts proceed from deliberately cultivated and deep-rooted habits. Ascetical theology looks to the development of *character*, a firm disposition for the good. Moral habits and ascetical virtues determine the character of any human being.

*Spiritual* theology looks to human behavior in the mode of *charity*, insofar as these good actions that proceed from deep-rooted habits are now directed to a personal *intimacy with God*. Human actions, at least in the Catholic and Christian sense, must have not only moral *content*, but spiritual *direction*. Some of the priests who abused young people may have never found this direction for their priestly lives. And *without that direction*, the priesthood can be a desolate and even bewildering existence, with depression, discouragement, and existential loneliness every step of the way. Of all the passions, sadness is the most destructive because when we are gripped by sadness and depression, we lose all hope and are open to any excess to relieve the sadness.

We, priests, have been trained for the best possible vocation on this earth. Most of us have a superb education. We have developed a wide range of remarkable skills, and most of us can hold our own with the best that the secular world has to offer: doctors, lawyers, statesmen, politicians, or corporate executives. Many of us have been given remarkable gifts that would be envied in any other profession. *But*, if those gifts, and the eminent elevated position that we hold, are not used for the glory of God, they can be put to any number of trivial, distracting, frivolous and self-serving uses.

A line in T. S. Eliot's *Murder in the Cathedral* puts this concept nicely:

> Servant of God has chance of greater sin
> Than the man who serves a king.
> For those who serve the greater cause
> May make the cause serve *them* ...[1]

I have known priests who spent more time hunting or fishing in Canada or taking vacations in the Bahamas than they did working in their parishes, or at least had no problem getting away whenever they wished. And I have known priests whose motor boat or sports car was more important to them than the modest lifestyle that was becoming their vocation. And I have also known priests who spent more time with their stock portfolios than they did with sacred study. We must admit that the priesthood provides the opportunity for a rather grand lifestyle if that is what we are really after.

We, priests, cannot simply be professionals among professionals, or administrators among administrators. We either become passionately involved with God, or we become passionately involved with prestige, pride of position, or trivial pursuits that merely amuse or entertain. Unless we are engaged with God on the deepest level of our beings, the bulk of our personal investment will be placed elsewhere, with very little return on the investment.

If the quality of our priestly lives is critical to our priesthood and our morale, something must be done about the priestly lifestyle itself so that we, priests, can have the privacy and the time that is needed for the cultivation of intimacy with God and the nourishment of our spiritual lives. Additionally, those in charge of seminary formation should be aware that asking a young man to give up the crowning act of his manhood, marriage, needs to be made worthwhile by offering the young man more than just a clerical identity. He needs the opportunity and the freedom to sacrifice himself for the moral and spiritual welfare of Christ's Bride, His Church. Apart from such an invitation, young men will, rightly, reject the life of a bachelor priest.

Needless to say, character and conscience require continuous firing in the crucible of prayer; otherwise, not only does our inner world become invaded by all kinds of useless worries, anxieties, and projections, but without prayer, we fall back upon our own meager resources and can feel desperately abandoned in our work and labors. Genuine prayer, because it is true communion with God, keeps expectations high. It prevents the lowering of expectations that often comes with "experience," the loss of idealism and vision that some look upon as "maturity." Often, too, clarity of purpose and forceful living are tempered with time and give way to less intense habits. When priestly expectations die, so does all true prayer. Mediocrity becomes the norm, and anything resembling a high expectation is looked upon as unrealistic. When and how this subtle substitution takes place is difficult to say, but that it does happen is evident in the lives of many priests and religious. I would like to lead you into the inner sanctum of priesthood, the remedy and antidote to those moments of depression and discouragement that often plague our days and are sometimes the open door to excesses of every kind.

To remedy such sadness, we need an artistry of the mind. By artistry of the mind, I mean a creative development of our theological skills, as well as an abiding in a theological culture. To live in such a culture, one immerses himself in *lectio divina*, a prayerful reading of the Word and the theologies that flow from this Word. As priests, we are called to cultivate the sanctity of the intellect. Preoccupation with God is the heart of the celibate commitment. We must be charmed, enchanted, delighted, absorbed, awed with God; and we must prepare our mind with a wealth of theological insights to nourish, sustain, enliven, and enrich this preoccupation.

The effect of this theological culture upon the mind of the priest cannot be overestimated. The human mind comes into living, vital contact with the eternal God, thereby acquiring an intellectual stability and perspective of incredible depth. By a strong passion of the mind, the priest acquires the ability to lean upon the truth of God and to educate himself to the true dimensions of reality and being. He is able to develop a wholesome *dependency* upon the God who abides in his mind and also a deep sense of *freedom* known in the truth that such a mind discovers. Moreover, this regular immersion in theological knowledge provides a solitude of spirit where the priest can find intimacy with

God in the midst of study and meditation. Theology becomes a shelter for the spirit, a space for intimacy and self-revelation, which are fertile ground for the development of deeper prayer.

One might think that this kind of study is only for saints, but the vocation to priesthood itself is shot through with a fantastic irony: *men* are invited to mediate *divine* truth and healing. No priest can escape this irony, nor can he escape the beauty of this call to live in a creative tension. "Yes, Lord, I, a man, will respond to Your divine call. Fill my mind with Your beauty." This dialectic, this tension between the human equation in priesthood and the untranslatable divine core, sets the man off into a direction of *dependent creativity* for rest of his days.

In Willa Cather's *Death Comes for the Archbishop*, Jean Baptiste Lamy arrives in Santa Fe as the new Bishop of this newly-acquired American territory to find that no one has ever heard of him. The priests in Santa Fe are under the jurisdiction of the Diocese of Durango in Mexico, and they have had no instructions to the contrary. The priests ask the Bishop about his credentials. Letters and documents had been sent to Durango, explaining the Bishop's purpose, but postal service in that part of the world was non-existent. What was the Bishop to do?

Then, the character of the Bishop comes through. After a few weeks of studying the situation in which he finds himself, and after having traveled a year to reach Santa Fe, he sets off alone on horseback to ride down to Mexico and back, a distance of three thousand miles, to retrieve his credentials. He could have turned back in utter discouragement and disillusionment—back even to his comfortable parish in Cincinnati, where he was respected and beloved by the people whom he served.

When the Bishop began his journey, he had no idea where Santa Fe was. The Bishop's friends advised him to go down the Mississippi River to New Orleans, then, by boat, to Galveston, across Texas to San Antonio, and then the long trek north through what the Mexicans called *El Paso del Norte*. His steamer wrecked in Galveston Bay, and he lost all of his worldly possessions, except for his books, which he had saved at the risk of his life. He crossed Texas in a traders' caravan, was almost killed when he had to jump from an overturning wagon, and had to lie for three months in the crowded house of a poor Irish family, waiting for his injured leg to heal.

In spite of him following trails that led nowhere, his running out of water, and his horse being exhausted, the Bishop experienced remarkable things on his journey. His spirits were lifted, and he truly felt like a priest, a man of God and a pastor of souls. One needs only to read Cather's book to see what guidance, comfort, and consolation God gives to his priests who are willing to offer their broken and limited humanity in service of divine truth and healing. Bishop Lamy's journey south, for all its hazards, difficulties, turns in the road that led nowhere, horses that faltered, and harrowing hours through deserts of sand was rewarding because he found people willing to trust him because he had first trusted the vocation itself—generously offering his humanity in service to God's love of creation. On his journey, he was welcomed by villages that had not seen a priest in decades; he baptized children, blessed marriages, celebrated Masses, and thanked God for the twists and turns in the road, for shipwrecks and Indian raids, and for the blessed providence that led him where he did not want to go and would not have gone if the mystery of his vocation had not demanded it.

When we find it difficult to obey God's will, when we would rather turn back and say, "It's not worth it," fields ripe for harvest rise before us, and we *know* that we are where God wants us to be. A life of character that willingly receives the grace of Christ is the true foundation for any priesthood and the rock-solid interior for carrying out our ministry, whatever that journey may bring.

We live in a soft society, a culture inured to comfort and ease. Often, we cannot tell the difference between an inconvenience and a disaster, and we can make every inconvenience *seem* like a disaster. Inconvenience and hardship are part of our work; difficult choices and, in some cultures, danger are built in to our vocation. Enduring hardships is not to make living martyrs out of us or to make us stoic and hardened men. We endure hardship out of love of Christ and His love for His people. No matter our failures and limits, or those of our brother priests, Christ is always offering the hope of renewal, of regeneration.

Thinking about human weakness reminds me of a scene in *Camelot*, the play about King Arthur and the dream of Camelot, a blessed kingdom of peace and justice, a kingdom seemingly destroyed by the infidelity of Guinevere and Lancelot. Likewise, all too recently, it seemed that the great dream of priesthood was all but destroyed by the faithlessness and betrayal of a few; and like Arthur, we stand thinking that the whole dream is over, the dream of priesthood and closeness to God that we had as young men when the priesthood beckoned us to happiness, to a meaningful and rich life. We, priests, can relate to the words that Arthur speaks:

> "Ask every person if he's heard the story:
> And tell it strong and clear if he has not:
> That once there was a fleeting glimpse of glory
> Called Camelot.
>
> Where once it never rained till after sundown;
> By eight a.m. the morning fog had flown,
> Don't let it be forgot
> That once there was a spot
> For one brief shining moment that was known
> As Camelot."[2]

The dream of cooperating in the mission of Christ never really dies because *He* sustains it in His own Person. With Him, in Him, and through Him, it will be born again in a new generation of young men who are beguiled by the spirit of self-giving. But we need to play our role and pass on the torch to another generation.

If only *one* young man is captured by the vision that we communicate to him about our priesthood, together we could be involved in raising a whole army of young knights who have the character and the temperament—born of prayerful study and deep engagement with the mystery of Christ—to make the Church come alive again. Priestly renewal has happened before. It will happen again—not for one brief, shining moment, but for a whole new age. This new age will be built upon sustained character transformation fostered within seminaries and the developing joy known in regular intimacy with the Trinity, an intimacy ever deepened by prayer, *by our character becoming prayer.*

121

# Notes

1    T.S. Eliot, *Murder in the Cathedral* (New York: Harcourt, Brace & World, 1963), 45.

2    Alan Jay Lerner and Frederick Loewe, *Camelot* (New York: Dell Publishing Company, 1967).

# Works Cited

Cather, Willa. *Death Comes For The Archbishop* (New York: Random House, 1990).

Eliot, T.S. *Murder in the Cathedral* (New York: Harcourt, Brace & World, 1963).

Lerner, Alan Jay and Frederick Loewe, *ed. Camelot* (New York: Dell Publishing Company, 1967).

Maritain, Jacques. *Art and Scholasticism* (London: Sheed & Ward, 1946).

Pieper, Josef. *The Cardinal Virtues* (South Bend, IN: Notre Dame University Press, 1966).

St. Thomas Aquinas. *Summa. Theologiae*, I-II, q. 37, ad 4.

St. Thomas Aquinas. *Summa. Theologiae*, II-II, 123, 12 ad 2.

St. Thomas Aquinas, *Treatise on the Virtues*, translated by John A. Oesterle (Notre Dame: University of Notre Dame Press, 1984).

# Sacramentum Tremendum

The year in which we, priests, are ordained to the priesthood is a year of grace. As we stand at that altar for the first time as a priest and are immersed in the marvel and mystery of the Eucharist, we are no longer the same man. From the moment of ordination, we are defined by our acting in *persona christi capitis*. Every time that the feast of Corpus Christi comes around, I ponder the great hymns of St. Thomas Aquinas. In magnificent language, these hymns capture the astonishing eucharistic reality that dwells among us, the heart and foundation of our priesthood and the primary and defining act of the priesthood of Jesus Christ.

As the dynamism of our priesthood and our identity, the eucharistic Christ must occupy the center of our hearts and minds. But is it really true, for us priests, that familiarity breeds contempt, or, at least, indifference and casualness as we stand at that altar? The whole meaning of the Incarnation is bound up with the mystery of the Eucharist, for that is where we meet our creator and redeemer in a personal and living intimacy. The Eucharist is the mystery of the Incarnation extended through time until it reaches us in the living fabric of our own life and existence. The Eucharist is either God in our midst, or it is nothing. A world where the God of the universe meets us in a loving communion and friendship is wondrous, indeed. Our world is vast, richer and deeper than the mysteries of science and human knowing. These human mysteries can only name something of His greatness, unable to contain the fullness of His presence communicated in the Eucharist.

How is it possible to express the intimacy with God that a priest experiences in the Eucharist? The Eucharist is the culmination of the priest's longing for God and the very crown of his priesthood. It is the final goal of his "aloneness," when his mind and spirit touch something of eternity and where God enfolds him in the garment of immortality. The Eucharist, bread that is flesh and flesh that is God, makes us priests; and it must be the source from which we draw our strength, our inspiration, our pastoral creativity, the insights by which we are led, and that hope which drives us on for a whole lifetime.

The destiny of every human being is intimacy with God in this life and in eternity, a matchless existence with God Himself. In the Eucharist, the priest touches upon that destiny in a special way and meets in conclave with the God who created him. There is nothing like this intimacy in the whole of human existence, and human words can only hesitatingly attempt to express its beauty and power:

> *Almighty God comes, in creation's God, man's Maker.*
>
> *Now must my thoughts dwell on deeps, render asunder the shell of things, and gazing through the bread, see God, and seeing God, let fall the curtains of my thoughts and dwell with God Who comes to me.*
>
> *For Christ comes, and all creation's doors swing back, and all eternal bells ring out: "Hosanna, Alleluia, Lord." The thanes in hell in horror*

*stop and feel the thunder of His Godhead, and burning spirits beings bend before a Mystery so deep. The culmination of creation, substance of our ancient Faith, nourishment of Christ's redeemed ones, bread that is flesh, and flesh that is God.*[1]

In this mystery especially, we grow from *notional* belief to *real* belief because in this mystery we really find the meaning and substance of human life. Pope John Paul II spent an hour in the presence of the Blessed Sacrament every morning before celebrating Mass. In quiet moments or in adoration before or after Mass, we are able to untangle some of our most critical and pressing human dilemmas. By this living communion, we are assured that we are not alone.

The Eucharist, St. Thomas says, *is the living evidence, the shining token of God's overpowering love for us. The very substance of our hope has its foundation in this tender familiarity of Christ toward us.* The Eucharist is proof of God's overwhelming love for us; and all of our hope is grounded in this closeness that we have with Christ in this amazing mystery. The Eucharist is not just a "sacrament," one of the many sacred rites of the Church within which we know and experience the effects of Christ's healing presence. In the Eucharist, Christ Himself comes into our very beings. We touch the very borders of eternity. The Eucharist is the event of deepest intimacy with God, the meeting place between man and God in this life, and a foreshadowing of eternal life, for which we are destined.

The Eucharist is the heart and center of the priest's intimacy with God, not only the center, but the intense furnace of his affective life and the laser-point of the meaning of his whole existence. The experience of the Eucharist is the living source of the indescribable joy that shakes his being to its very depths and keeps him continually conscious of the magnitude of God. In the celebration of the Eucharist, pondering the dimensions of this mystery, the inward eye is opened and the moral gaze is sharpened and made fully aware. This mystic communion with God and our own openness to savor the full meaning of what we encounter digs a deep world of interiority. From this life of priestly interiority comes a persistent sharing in Christ's own spousal self-giving to the Church.

If a man really enters that furnace of being, something of its marvel and wonder rubs off on him and roots him in a joy that he cannot possibly conceal. The *manner* of celebrating the Eucharist that emerges from this encounter is transformed. Because a priest's manner of celebration reveals for himself and for those whom he leads in worship the *mysterium tremendum*, the consciousness of those for whom he celebrates can be deepened as his prayerful disposition betrays an inner being awestruck in adoration. By his manner, the priest invites the congregation to meditate upon the great nuptial act of Christ, an act offered to all people in all ages: "This is my body, which will be given for you" (Lk. 22:19).

Is it too much to ask that we, priests and bishops, acquire sensitivity in matters of eucharistic celebration and understand the critical role of the priest-celebrant in savoring the mysteries of God? For that is quite literally what the celebration of the Eucharist is: the savoring of the mystery of God's self-donative love. A dialectic of manner and meaning is present in the priest's liturgical action: The meaning should define and shape the manner, and the manner should embody and reveal the meaning of the mystery celebrated.

The full power of our priestly character should point toward the mystic element in the liturgical act. The priest-celebrant is the dispenser of the mysteries of God, and his own savoring of them in the act of worship helps to make them "visible" to the worshiping community. The intensity and clarity of his faith in the celebration of the Eucharist is a powerful factor in making the parish liturgy a truly transforming experience. The more that the priest-celebrant becomes the visible expression of the invisible realities he encounters, the more powerful is his priestly role in the act of worship. The manner is a vehicle by which the meaning of the sacred rite is communicated.

In 1941, the Welsh Catholic poet and artist David Jones was living in Kensington, England, just outside of London, and he typically attended Mass at a Carmelite church in the area. The church was later destroyed by bombing, and Jones was so moved by the sight of the bombed church that he wrote a poem called *The Kensington Mass*. In it, he tried to capture the significance of the Mass for himself and for the people of Europe, devastated by a terrible war. He saw the Mass as the hope of humanity, the heart of the Church's mission to humanity, and one of the few things of beauty in a war-torn world.

Jones saw the Mass as the central Christian mystery, summing up the whole of the European tradition of civilization and culture, a Europe which was, at the time, being blown apart by the most terrible war in history. And he saw the Mass and the Eucharist, which is God's presence in the world, capable of making all things new when the destruction of the war was gone, the fire and wind of the Holy Spirit bringing all peoples together around the sacred ritual of the altar.

After the war, Jones began what is considered his masterpiece, a very difficult, book-length poem called *Anathamata*. In language filled with allusions to history and to Catholic doctrine, he drew out the wonder of the Mass, reaching back through the legend of the Holy Grail to the very wellsprings of Western civilization itself. The poem is not easy reading, but for those who are patient and willing to struggle with odd turns of phrase and strange imagery, it gives a magnificent vision of God's presence in human history and the transforming power of the Mass.

Jones shows how the words and actions of the Mass evoke the Christian memory and the history of salvation, taking us back to the early ages of the Church when the Mass was celebrated in catacombs and over the tombs of martyrs. Every age of Catholic history has added to the ritual of the Mass, and the very words *Kyrie* or *Gloria* or *agios_ô_theos* of the ancient chants give us a unity with the Catholics who have gone before us who said the same words and sang the same chants. By the power and centuries-old endurance of the Mass, God hovers over humanity, taking to Himself the cares and hopes of the world; the Mass is security and stability in a changing world.

In 1947, Jones began another project, this time a painting. He wanted to create a visual counterpart of his

*Kensington Mass*, the picture of a bombed-out Carmelite church; and he came up with a startling painting which he later named *a latere dextro*, taken from the Easter liturgy, wherein we hear of the water flowing from the right side of the Temple, bringing saving waters to humanity. The central figure in the painting is a priest offering Mass, the chalice held high, altar boys with candles and incense, and an image of the crucified Christ in the background. The painting is mystical, filled with David Jones's belief in the Mass bringing hope to the world.

From his experience of two world wars, David Jones became aware that the Church is the only stable force in human life and in human civilization. The Church's eternal mission is carried on and symbolized by the Mass, born from the side of the Savior as Eve was born of Adam. The death of Christ sums up the suffering of redeemed humanity, the martyrs who shed their own blood in the face of persecution, the bombed-out churches that are relics of the Church's mission to humanity, the candles and crosses and incense that speak of heavenly things, and the altar and chalice around which humanity gathers. In the darkness of war, David Jones felt the power of the Catholic faith and the exhilarating hope that the Mass gave him in the midst of ruin and destruction, a power and a hope that not even the bombed-out Carmelite church could obliterate. Here was something enduring through time and eternity, and he recognized that the stability for which the world was searching was contained in the Mass.

Can our vision of the Mass and our conviction of its meaning be any less as we stand at the altar, with visions of priests of the past standing around altars and lifting up the cup of sacrifice and boys with tall candles kneeling in awe of their Maker, or have we reduced Mass to a mere obligation to be dispensed with before the really important business of the day begins? Could any words be more expressive of the priest's thoughts and feelings in the midst of the Real presence of God than these famous words of St. Thomas Aquinas?

> *Godhead, here in hiding whom I do adore,*
> *Masked by the bare shadows, shape and nothing more.*
> *See, Lord, at Thy service low lies here a heart*
> *Lost, all lost in wonder at the God Thou art.*
>
> *Jesu, Whom I gaze on shrouded here below*
> *I beseech Thee send me what I thirst for so:*
> *Someday to gaze on Thee, face to face in light,*
> *And be blessed forever with Thy glory's sight.*
> *Oro fiat illud guod tam sitio...* [2]

We must not only believe the doctrine with our mind, but we must enter into the mystery to which the doctrine points, a mystery in which we are essentially immersed as priests.

I encourage the priests of my diocese to spend one hour before the Blessed Sacrament each day. It is surprising what a stabilizing and quieting time that is and how many ideas light up in one's head for furthering priestly work. At first, it may seem that we have nothing to say to God with our minds completely blank. But after a while, if we open our hearts in faith and truth, we have plenty to think about and receive from the very source of our priesthood, Jesus Christ. Sometimes, lighting two candles and exposing the Eucharist in a monstrance helps me to ponder in His Presence.

Many serious and pressing problems have been solved that way. Time spent in adoration is never lost. Those who cultivate this habit will be astonished at how much they receive from it.

In 1264, Pope Urban IV gathered around himself the great minds and scholars of the Church to grapple with the serious problems the Church was facing and to make the Catholic heritage a viable force in the Mediterranean world. The world was divided between Christians and Moslems; and Christians were divided between Catholics and Orthodox. Pope Urban had assigned the young Thomas Aquinas to study and find a solution to many of these problems of division. Aquinas, at the time, was deep in his Greek studies from which would emerge some of his greatest works, but these studies were interrupted, temporarily, by another commission from the Pope—to draw upon his theological knowledge to compose the Mass and Office for a new feast of the Eucharist, a feast that would become our feast of Corpus Christi.

The great theologian poured the wealth of Catholic teaching on the Eucharist into that Mass and Office. He also composed, in lucid and stirring Latin, a whole treasure of eucharistic hymns, which the Catholic people sing even to this day. The cool, rational Aquinas wrote glowing poetry and mystic cadences as he captured in living language the wonder and marvel of the Eucharist, God's living Presence among His people. The latin of the First Vespers Hymn set the pace with its stately language and stirring rhythm:

*Pange lingua Gloriosi*
*Corporis mysterium,*

131

*Sanguinisque pretiosi*
*Quem in mundi pretium*
*Fructus ventris generosi*
*Rex effudit gentium.*

The song ended with the verses that every Catholic has sung during the traditional Benediction rite: the *Tantum Ergo*:

*Down before so deep a Mystery*
*Let our beings lowly bow;*
*Ancient rites pass into history,*
*Newly-formed our worship now.*
*Faith gains insight to the Mystery*
*Which the senses cannot know.*

The words and the theology are pure adoration as St. Thomas draws out the meaning of this "memorial of our redemption": Christ dwells among us, really and personally, and we fall in adoration before, "Bread that is flesh and flesh that is God." This God comes into our very beings, to be with us as the companion of all of our days, to plant within us the seed of everlasting life. The Eucharist is a Mystery to be *cultivated*: Eucharistic *belief* must grow into eucharistic *consciousness*. Empty belief in the Eucharist is not enough, for such belief can easily lead to a sterile faith. The awe and wonder must grow and deepen as we celebrate the mystery again and again. As priests, we are privileged to enter into this mystery again and again, bringing with us our love of Christ and His love for His Bride, the Church.

# Notes

1    Reverend Clifford Stevens, *Rain From My Roots* (Denver, CO: Peartree Press, 1991).

2    *Manual of Prayers*, Gerard Manley Hopkins, S.J., *ed.* (Chicago: Midwest Theological Forum, 2005) 375-376.

# Works Cited

Allchin, A.M. *The World is a Wedding* (New York: Crossroad Publishing Company, 1982) 117.

Jones, David. *The Kensington Mass.*

Jones, David. *Anathemata* (Boston: Faber and Faber, 1952).

Pope Pius XII, *Mediator Dei*, 1947.

St. Thomas Aquinas. *Devoutly I Adore Thee: The Prayers and Hymns of St. Thomas Aquinas*, Johann Moser, Robert Anderson, *ed.* (Manchester, NH: Sophia Institute Press).

Stevens, Clifford. *Rain From My Roots* (Denver, CO: Peartree Press, 1991).

# Theotokos

When Henry Adams, a non-Catholic, explored the ancient abbey of Mont Saint-Michel off the coast of Normandy, he was astonished by the role of Mary in medieval life and even more astonished when he discovered the Cathedral of Chartres some time later. Mary's presence in Catholic life amazed him, and he saw her as more than a historical figure who moves through the Gospels. He rightly understood that she was a living embodiment of human aspiration toward God.

But Henry Adams experienced only a tiny glimpse of that reality, of the human aspiration for God that Mary embodies and nourishes. Chartres and Mont Saint-Michel sought to capture in stone and stained glass the heights to which the human spirit can soar in its ascent to God. They are monuments to the glory of God and to the human spirit which aspires to God. As visible works of art, they express the invisible, making the life of the spirit incarnate in matter. Adams was surprised to discover that Mary, herself, was the inspiration for these works, for she made incarnate in her womb the Son of God Himself. By her assent to be the Mother of God, she opened the floodgates of the Spirit to lead the whole human race to the heights of glory.

So that is where we must start in any talk of the Mother of God, the *Theotokos*, as the Greeks loved to call her, with that *assent* to a destiny that were unsought and unexpected, but which fashioned and shaped her person, as our own assent to the priesthood fashions and shapes our person. If we are to have a real devotion to Mary, we must imitate that assent which made her who she is, just as our call to the priesthood, once we assent to it, makes us who we are. Meditating from time to time upon all that such an assent entails is important. Our assent is more than lying on the Cathedral floor before the Bishop when we are ordained or answering, "Present," when our name is called in ordination. Assent means that from the moment we accept, our whole life is embodied in the priesthood and in collaborating with Jesus Christ for the salvation of the world.

Before giving my own assent to a priestly vocation, I spent a year in prayer and gave myself to contemplation, looking at what I was considering. I realize now how important that time was, because everything I would put my hands to as a priest would stem from the freedom of that future assent. The assent to priesthood is *our part* in the vocation; and half-hearted, half-conscious assent will never do.

We see here, again, the power of interiority, of that deep communion with Christ where we habitually dwell. In interior communion with God, we experience the workings of God's presence in all of its terrifying majesty. Drawn by Him who shapes our call in us, we are drawn to agreement with Him, finding ourselves, in a sense, *inside* the providential act and receiving its intimate truth: "you are a priest forever" (Ps. 110:4).

The assent of which I speak and which I would like you to examine and reaffirm is something into which the whole content of your being enters; it leavens your whole existence, deepening and developing every religious instinct that you have ever had. The assent is very similar to that given by the Blessed Mother.

Mary is bound up in the Incarnation and Resurrection of the Son of God. At the Annunciation, Mary becomes the lone observer of the mystery of Christ's person and His origin. She is the co-laborer of the Holy Spirit in God's greatest task in time: the enfleshment of God Himself. Her "yes" is bound up essentially with the very *rationale* of redemption. Moreover, and this is the point for us in our priestly assent, *she was not just a passive instrument.* Her whole being bent to His intentions. Every human faculty and every divine gift was engaged in this mighty task; and she, thus, became the model for all who seek God, for she was a conscious, living instrument of God's will.

A certain *knowing* of God accompanies entering into His will, and that entering into His will gives us access to the hidden God. Our call to the priesthood is, in a sense, God revealing Himself to us. By our assent, we not only submit ourselves to His intentions; we align ourselves with them. We are no longer merely passive instruments in His hands. Like Mary, we bend our whole beings to His intentions, every human faculty and every inherited gift absorbed in the task to which He has called us. We, too, become a conscious, living instrument of His will. Mary's complete availability to the divine will constitutes her character. Our assent to the divine will does not mean that we are putty in the hands of God; it means that we are ready to carry out with all of the powers within us, with the entire wealth of our human faculties and affective life, the priestly and pastoral tasks to which we have been called.

Pope Paul VI had a peculiar dislike for ephemeral sentimentalism masquerading as devotion to Mary, a "vain credulity, which substitutes reliance on merely external practices for serious commitment," which does not lead to "persevering and practical action" (*Marialis Cultus* 38). Mary is a tough model. "[W]hile completely devoted to the will of God," Pope Paul VI wrote, she "was far from being a timidly submissive woman or one whose piety was repellent to others" (*MC* 37).

Most people are unfamiliar with the *Medici Madonna* of Michelangelo. Quite different from traditional Madonnas, it betrays a strength and toughness not usually associated with figures of Mary. In the sculpture, the Child Jesus is turning back to Mary, and she is viewing Him somewhat sternly, holding Him firmly in her grasp. Pope Paul VI is reminding us of this image of Mary as the strong woman, the concerned and involved woman, the spiritual *Mother of Courage* who is part of the human drama; and he says that when we begin to understand Mary, she will *appear not as a mother exclusively concerned with her own Divine Son, but as a woman whose action helped to strengthen the apostolic community's faith in Christ, and whose maternal role was extended and became universal on Calvary.*

We, priests, have to enter into a real devotion to Mary within our hearts. To do so, we have to possess something of the toughness that characterized the Mother of Jesus herself. Mary celebrates the immortality of every single human being: created by God, redeemed by God, and destined for a matchless existence in eternal life. She proclaims by her very person that human life opens into eternity and that the wonder of the Incarnation is part of the drama of every human life. Mary keeps alive a vision of human worth, pointing us toward our freedom to cooperate with the providential will of God or resisting its terrible beauty in our solitary "no."

Devotion to Mary means belief in the Incarnation, in the wonder of God becoming man, and in that deep spirit of adoration which gives stability to our own existence and leads us to say, "yes" to an adventure with God. The mission of Christ leads us to the very fabric of life: to share the Good News with everyone. We are free in our "yes" to God to labor in love to satisfy His thirst for souls. We call upon Mary to assist us with her prayers, prayers that carry a woman's love for men who think not of themselves but of the welfare of the Bride. We can continue to meditate on the words of Pope John Paul II in 1998 in his Holy Thursday Letter to priests:

> The priest is called to match the *fiat* of Mary at all times, allowing himself to be led by the Spirit as she was ... Accompanied by Mary, the priest will be able to renew his consecration day after day; and the time will come when, trusting the guidance of the Spirit whom he has invoked on his journey as man and as priest, he will set forth upon the ocean of light which is the Trinity.

# Works Cited

Adams, Henry. *Mont St. Michel and Chartres* (Boston: Houghton, Mifflin Company, 1912).

Pope John Paul II, "Holy Thursday Letter," 1998.

Pope Paul VI, *Marialis Cultus*, 1974.

*Prayer to the Virgin of Chartres* in *The Golden Book of Catholic Poetry,* ed. Alfred Noyes (New York: J.B. Lippincott, 1946).

Stevens, Clifford. *The Blessed Virgin Mary* (Our Sunday Visitor Press, 1985), 91-94.

# Grappling with the Sacred Text

I have an image of John Paul II, during his days as Bishop and Cardinal, sitting at this small desk in front of the Blessed Sacrament in his private chapel, grappling with the text of the Scriptures, trying to wring from it the insights and meanings for his priestly and pastoral work. We know from John Paul II's series of talks on the *Theology of the Body* how deeply he had penetrated the meaning and substance of a few passages in Genesis and in the Gospels and how he was able to draw out of them brilliant insights and applications. In this, he showed himself as something of a new Father of the Church, laying the groundwork for a resurgent Christian culture: the new evangelization.

The great achievement of the Greek Fathers—St. Basil, St. Gregory Nazianzus, and St. Gregory Nyssa—was that from their intense penetration of the Scriptures, they were able to create a uniquely Christian culture in the midst of raging paganism and political savagery. The letters of St. Gregory Nazianzus and St. Basil illustrate the saints' theological and pastoral genius at work. Comparing the entries in a classical Greek lexicon with those in a patristic Greek lexicon illustrates how these saints changed the very meaning of Greek classical concepts and gave those concepts a uniquely Christian context.

As pastors, if we are really serious about transforming, nourishing, and enriching the lives of our people, we must be immersed in the Scriptures; and, like our own chief pastor and those early Christian Fathers who fashioned a

Christian civilization, we too must grapple with the sacred texts. The Scriptures yield amazing and startling insights into pastoral labors. John Henry Newman, who carried on a unique pastoral work in the nineteenth century and who left us a wealth of insight into priestly and pastoral work, wrote these insightful lines:

> There is no greater mistake, surely, than to suppose that a revealed truth precludes originality in the treatment of it ... reassertions of what is old with a luminousness of explanation of the new, is a gift inferior only to that of revelation itself.[1]

If today's preaching is suffering from anything, it is a lack of living contact with the truth-bearing images of Scriptures, from which preaching has always drawn its realism and vitality. The problem seems to be twofold: the mistaking of *Biblicism* for preaching and the common temptation to reduce the whole of preaching to exhortation. *Biblicism* is simply a naked commentary on the text, something that a congregation does not really need, since they have heard the text hundreds of times before. And mere moral exhortation reduces preaching to something resembling a nagging mother.

Newman, in his own preaching, recognized the complexity of the Scriptures and the strong temptation to make a sermon a mere naked repetition of the text, for which the hearer does not need a preacher. He recognized that the preacher receives insight into the Scriptural text from prayer and study and must make these insights part of his own mind and heart. After this reception, the preacher can communicate the insights to someone else.

Newman's genius is contained in his *Parochial and Plain Sermons* and in his *University Sermons.* He had the ability to give his hearers a mirror of the Scriptural teaching in which *they* could view *themselves* in the concrete circumstances of their lives. We can simply read the titles of these sermons to see how deeply Newman penetrated into the text and its startling application for a particular audience. He used no rhetorical devices, and he scarcely raised his voice, but his masterly grasp of the application of a particular text to an audience was often breathtaking. Even the inflection of his voice was remembered years later.

Newman was also convinced of another reality that preachers often miss, something having nothing to do with style or manner of delivery but in the *intellectual* preparation which the preacher must bring to the text. The freshness of preaching is found precisely in the preacher's knowledge of his audience, of the circumstances in which they live, and in those modes of speech which will penetrate their minds and hearts. Much preaching simply misses the listeners, saying little to them personally.

Newman also knew that there was a far greater challenge in preaching than the simple explication of the text: the need to find the thread of God's intentions through the text. The loving will of God must come through in the preaching, a will diverse for each one of the hearers but bound up in the text. Newman was a keen observer of everything around him, of the happenings of his own times, of the movements that affected the world in which he lived, of the major figures of the day, and of the chief influences upon society. And so his preaching was not shooting in the dark; it was not the mere mouthing of a sacred text. He brought that text to his hearers in language they could understand, to face the problems that *they* had to face.

One of the geniuses of the sacred text is that it has a unique meaning and application for each one of us. We can see this flexibility of application in our praying of the psalms. At times, I have been astonished at what I have prayed in the *Liturgy of the Hours*. Sometimes, it seems that a text was placed there especially for me, so real is its force and meaning for me at that particular time.

Since the inner fabric of the priestly psyche is essentially *theological*, the *esse* and the *ethos* of this psyche must be rooted in prayerful contemplation of revelation. These penetrations of the divine genius must somehow alloy with the basic ore of the priestly identity, giving it a rich treasure of thought, obtainable from no other source. The mind that is not stirred by revelation must ultimately find a cheaper alloy, and history records the watering down of the priestly identity in ages as various as tenth century in Rome and seventeenth century in France. In both circumstances, the study of Scripture was at a low ebb.

To be in contact with the living Word of God does not mean, as is so often stated, a mere "meditative reading" of the sacred text, a mere familiarity with the sacred writings. It can mean the intellectual *shattering* of our prejudices, biases, and intuitions, and the welcoming of the Spirit's work in re-assimilating the fabric of our mind. In the study of Scripture, no two journeys are alike, since each man penetrates divine truth with his own equivalent of the pick and shovel. Sadly, many priests have never known the exhilaration of Scriptural discovery or the personally transforming experience of this act of discovery.

By this act of entering Scripture study, our priestly identity is made more secure and clear, just as the eye can be activated to its own proper act by contact with light. When I was a seminarian at Louvain, I went to the Holy Land with classmates; we backpacked around the Sea of Galilee, reading the Gospel of Mark. Reading the Gospel in that setting and with total vulnerability to its Truth forever transformed my experience of reading the Gospel. The memories triggered by that text always elicit the desire to once again be open to the complete spiritual immersion I knew during my experience in the Holy Land. The Scriptures embody the *action of God upon human history*, an action which has not ceased and will not cease until the end of time. The Scriptures are not merely an account of God's actions in the past but also the occasion of His action upon human history *now*. By grappling with the sacred text, we begin to discern the thread of God's intentions in the present; and in our preaching, we are able to communicate His truth to our hearers.

The prime value for the priest in grappling with the sacred text is found in his openness to the words, which speak intimately to his mind and heart. This intimacy is not for the priest alone but is destined to elicit life in his parishioners as the homily is expressed as a prayerful invitation. God is the master of history and the master of the human heart, and He has fashioned His word in such a way that we find what we need with a concreteness that is uncanny.

One remarkable explanation of the genius of the Word of God is articulated in a commentary by St. Ephraim of Syria, one of the great Fathers of the early Church:

> Lord, who can grasp the wealth of just one of Your words. What we understand is much less than what we leave behind, like thirsty people who drink from a fountain. For Your word, Lord, has many shades of meaning, just as those who study it have many different points of view. The Lord has colored his words with many hues, so that each person who studies it can see in it what applies to him. He has hidden many treasures in His word so that each of us is enriched as we ponder it.[2]

These words do not mean that some secret meaning is to be found in Scripture, hidden there just for us. Rather, they indicate that the Word of God is so rich that it can reach us in the concrete circumstances of our own life. The Word of God is like a diamond with countless facets, that as we turn it, we find that it has meaning for us in our own particular situation. Sometimes, the meaning is so particular to my needs that it is breathtaking and life-changing.

We do not have to be specialists in Sacred Scripture to find meaning in it, although a good supply of commentaries by dedicated scholars can be of great help to us. We all have our own tastes and preferences for research, and we should build up our own library to help us to explore the Scriptures. But when all is said and done, it is the words, themselves, with which we have to grapple. We are dealing not just with another written text, but with the very Word of God, intended to change our hearts and then deepen and develop our moral character. The Fathers of the Church were not Scriptural specialists according to the meaning that we attach to the word *specialist* today; yet, because they were pastors and shepherds of souls, they were able to draw out the meaning of the Word of God for their flocks with eloquence and power that still ring through their writings. The exposition of Scripture was considered part of their pastoral care, and their familiarity with the Word of God is awe-inspiring.

This grappling with the Word of God is also an antidote to the dominant cultural voices in newspapers, magazines, motion pictures, television, the Internet, and radio. Through these mediums, we encounter people whose world vision is far different from our own. Ours is not a religious culture, and Christian and Catholic values find little encouragement in this economically-driven, popular culture. In a sense, we have to create our own culture, our own environment, where God is dominant and where fidelity and loyalty to Him is the prime commitment, hoping that such fidelity will affect the secular culture.

Part of living the priesthood is a matter of not permitting our Catholic vision to be eroded by the pagan culture that we inhabit. The ancient practice of *lectio divina*, mentioned by Pope John Paul II in his Apostolic Letter *Novo Millennio Ineunte*, is the habit of cultivating and scheduling a constant contact with the Scriptures, with at least as much fervor with which we watch a fine motion picture, the Super Bowl, or some other stunning public event. The Word of God does not permit us to escape from the world and the culture in which we live, and it would be foolish to try to do so. But we can *penetrate* that culture with the wisdom of the Word and the genius of the revealed text, keeping before our eyes the radical demands of the Gospel.

> There is no doubt that primacy of holiness and prayer is inconceivable without a renewed *listening to the word of God*. Ever since the Second Vatican Council underlined the pre-eminent role of the word of God in the life of the Church, great progress has certainly been made in the devout listening to Sacred Scripture and the attentive study of it. . . . It is especially necessary that listening to the word of God should be a life-giving encounter ... draw[ing] from the Biblical text the living word which questions, directs and shapes our lives (*NMI* 39).

# Notes

1    John Henry Newman, *Historical Sketches, The Benedictine School*, section 5.

2    St. Ephraim of Syria, *Commentary on the Diatessaron*, found in the Roman Breviary, 2nd Reading for Sunday of the 6th Week of Ordinary Time.

# Works Cited

*A Patristic Greek Lexicon,* G. W. H. Lampe, D.D., ed. (Oxford: Clarendon Press, 1961).

Newman, John Henry. *Historical Sketches*, Vol. 2: *The Benedictine School* (London: Longmans, Greens & Co., 1906).

Newman, John Henry. *Parochial and Plain Sermons* (San Francisco: Ignatius Press, 1997).

Pope John Paul II, *Theology of the Body: Human Love in the Divine Plan* (Boston: Pauline Media & Books, 1997).

Pope John Paul II, *Novo Millenio Ineunte*, 2001.

St. Ephraim of Syria, *Commentary on the Diatessaron*, in the Roman Breviary, 2nd Reading for Sunday of the 6th Week of Ordinary Time.

# Keepers of the Flame

At the time of his ordination, every priest, in a sense, is in a land without any maps; he is in uncharted territory. Every priest must make for himself the maps and the charts that will lead him into the great unknown, the future that lies before him in the priesthood. He has no idea what lies before him in his first assignment, but that does not matter. What matters is his firm determination that nothing can discourage him because he is committed to continually receiving into his heart the great love that God has for him. This capacity for receptivity keeps the flame of his priesthood burning with confident power.

Living out of the power of this truth will make all the difference in our priesthood: God dwells in me as love; therefore, I never want to leave this dwelling. In light of this truth, we have to believe that our vocation makes a difference, that we have been called by Jesus Christ, Himself, to labor for Him in a definite and specific vineyard and that we have been formed and equipped in splendid fashion to conquer the world for Christ. If our expectations are low, we will never rise above mediocrity. If our expectations are high, our will becomes vulnerable to grace and Christ can accomplish great things in our ministry.

A priest needs to be idealistic. Explicitly or implicitly, the priest will be asked by contemporary culture to accept mediocrity as his goal and to be satisfied with his mediocre second-best. The real horror will be if the priest accepts mediocrity *for himself*; as soon as he takes mediocrity for himself, his spiritual life withers. We are the heirs of a four-hundred-year-old Catholic priesthood on this continent, and we follow in the footsteps of remarkable men who have carved out a Church in what was once but a barren wilderness. I remember reading the journals of Father De Smet, the great Jesuit, the famous Blackrobe, who roamed the plains of the western United States less than two hundred years ago and who wrote of what the future might be here. He saw great cities arising and huge populations inhabiting the wilderness. Our task is different; we are called to be pioneers by finding new ways to bring the Gospel to people who, in some respects, have grown old in their religion, expecting very little from it. For them, religion is a leisure activity, and they are unwilling to invest themselves substantially. Rather, the faith is something relegated to their spare time. *We are called to be a light to such people and to help them make religion the center of their lives.*

St. Elizabeth Ann Seton was certainly one of the bright lights. In 12 years, from 1809 to 1821, she founded the Sisters of Charity, laid the foundation for the parochial school system in the United States, wrote textbooks, trained her Sisters in the best teaching methods, founded orphanages, worked among the poor and the sick, sent her Sisters across the country doing every kind of good work, and died with plans in her hands for even greater things. Elizabeth Ann Seton is proof that we do not have to be satisfied with just treading water and merely keeping the ship of the Church afloat. A man does not become a priest to merely inhabit the future. He becomes a priest because important work has been entrusted to him.

St. Joseph Cafasso, a priest of the last century, lived in the industrial city of Torino in Italy. He became the spiritual advisor and friend of many priests, among them, the young Don Bosco. Father Cafasso enflamed these young priests with his own zeal and vision of priesthood, brought about a spiritual revolution in Torino, and took on the most difficult mission in the diocese—chaplain to the prisons. When Don Bosco, in a crisis of conscience, wanted to volunteer for the foreign missions, Father Cafasso told him: "Go home and unpack your bags; we need you here in Italy!" And we know what St. John Bosco accomplished in his lifetime.

Priests of today are the heralds of the new evangelization proclaimed by Pope John Paul II. We are, in a sense, missionaries to a world that does not know God and that does not want to know God. We should not think that our own people are unaffected by the secularism around them. They are immersed in it; they breathe its air every day; they need the clear and bracing air of the Gospel that we have been entrusted to communicate to them.

The Church is in a difficult period, as is humanity itself, and the strongest voice of hope in the midst of this period is the one who sits in the chair of Peter and views the whole world from that height. We live in a time of spiritual danger which carries the following threats:

1. Practical atheism: those who believe in God but who do not really believe in the power of prayer

2. Practical materialism: those who do not really believe in divine providence

3. Practical paganism: a complete eclipse of the eternal in the practical business of living

We, priests, are not exempt from these dangers, but the priesthood itself, the very presence of priests in the world, is one of the great antidotes to these dangers. Often, we are not aware of the power of our presence, of our persons, and of how the whole climate of a room or of a gathering can change when we walk into it. Such change has nothing to do with our humble persons in themselves, but that we are priests and we represent something greater than ourselves.

I have a friend who was chaplain at an Air Force Base in New Mexico when President John F. Kennedy was assassinated in 1963. He was the only priest on base and, like the rest of the country, was in a state of shock at this great tragedy. But that evening, he decided to make the rounds of the clubs on base where people would be gathered to talk about the shocking events of that day: the Airmen's Club, the Non-Commissioned Officers Club, the Civilian Club, and the Officers Club. He was astonished to find that he was welcomed like an angel from heaven.

My friend did not realize it, but as a priest, the only priest on base, he was the living symbol of stability in the midst of the shock and uncertainty of that day. He remarked that he had never realized the power of the priesthood more than on that day. His very presence brought strength, comfort, healing, and a sense of stability at a time when the whole world seemed to be falling apart.

We can begin to live in a very small world, confined by the boundaries of our diocese, our deanery, or even our parish, and begin to have small thoughts and small feelings and even small expectations for our priesthood. We can fail to realize that we represent the world's stability and that the vocation and virtue we wear says more than a thousand sermons. *We* are the presence of God and His Church in the world, and we must not let any scandal, any negative publicity, or any bad public climate make us forget the beauty and power of our call. Without good and holy shepherds, the Church will be scattered to the four winds.

Father Daniel Berrigan, the Jesuit poet, speaks of a crucifix on a Quebec roadside that had become the symbol of the world's stability for the hard-working farming people of that region, the "burning glass" that held "crops, houses and men, in its fire ... more permanent than any mountain that time could bring down."[1] The vocation to priesthood is shot through with a fantastic irony; God uses the finite to lift others into the infinite. The tension between the human equation in priesthood and the divine core that defies all human mathematics is bound up with the very nature of priesthood. We do not represent *ourselves*, however brilliant our minds or scintillating our personalities, however towering our achievements or broad our influences.

Two seminarians from Budapest went for a hike into the mountains around the city, and they came across a small church in the wilderness where a priest was pastor to a small village on the edge of nowhere. They found the priest digging turnips in his small garden, and after a few moments, one of the young men said to him:
"Don't you feel alone and insignificant in your little church out here in the middle of nowhere? Doesn't it make you feel unimportant?"

"Young man," the priest said, "The Jesus in my tabernacle is the same Jesus down there in your great cathedral in Budapest." And he continued to dig for his turnips.

155

This tension between our human finitude and the greatness of the divine can be sensed in the bewildering groping of the ancient Hebrew prophets, scrawling their message from God in cryptic accents that, in Hebrew, ring with a finality that tore their beings apart. It can also be seen in a lesser way in a Joan of Arc, who listened to God's voice, heeded it, yet had to accept a final destruction as the crowning act of her fidelity. The soul-searing nature of priesthood carries with it the possibility of immense tragedy and incredible joy, and every priest is marked with a joy that shines through every nerve and muscle of his clumsy self or with a tragedy that marks him as one who surrenders and entrusts his ministry to the mystery of Christ now dwelling with him. Without this surrendering to God, the demands of this world, and even of our own bodies, can be too much to resist. The example of our brother-priests who dared to turn to the dark side of their human personalities is a powerful confirmation of this phenomenon.

This tension in priesthood can be resolved only by a living and vibrant concept of the priesthood itself. The elements of that concept must be drawn from the living tradition of the priesthood in the Church, in its many varieties and roles down through the centuries, and expressed in the living language of the mind. Reason must be stirred to grapple with the concrete historical context in which a priest finds himself and to find new facets in the priestly identity to answer the present need. We are living expressions of the human and the divine in the priesthood, and our pastoral labors will give expression to that tension in different ways.

We, priests, should not be surprised when we face the unexpected, perhaps even the unwished for and unwanted. We have no idea what the future will hold for us, and God is not going to consult *us* about what He allows to enter our lives. We can become very secure, very content, and very comfortable in our pastoral assignments; and we can become lazy and stale and very neat in the little nests that we have made for ourselves.

Priesthood as an unexpected adventure of trust is characterized by the life of St. Turibius de Mogrovejo. He was a brilliant young law student at the University of Salamanca in Spain in the sixteenth century, and he later became an even more brilliant professor. He was noticed by King Philip II of Spain, who made him chief judge of the ecclesiastical court at Granada. Turibius de Mogrovejo expected to remain in this position for the rest of his life. But suddenly, his whole life went in another, totally unexpected and even unwanted, direction. The Archbishopric of Lima, Peru in New Spain became vacant, and against all his protests and every precedent, he was appointed Archbishop in that far, distant land. He was 42 years old.

What Turibius de Mogrovejo found in Lima was utter social, political, economic, and religious chaos. The Spanish colonists gave only lip-service to their religion; slavery of the native Peruvians was everywhere. Immorality was pervasive. The greed for gold was the motor of the whole society, and the country had not yet recovered from the slaughter of the native Incas by Pizarro and his fellow conquistadors. Turibius de Mogrovejo's diocese embraced the high mountains of the Andes range, some of the peaks rising over 20,000 feet, with villages and grazing lands which had never seen a priest. He saw only violence and immorality on every side, and he set about fighting injustice and vice, poverty and oppression, bringing down upon himself the hatred of Spanish officials who were little more than murderers and thieves.

Turibius de Mogrovejo made a seven-year pastoral visitation of his diocese, never returning to Lima in all that time. He supported and inspired others, like St. Martin de Porres, St. Rose of Lima, and Blessed Juan Massias to carry on in his spirit, and he succeeded in rooting out the most flagrant moral and legal abuses within his diocese. He lived by this dictum: "Christ said, 'I am the Truth'; He did not say, 'I am the custom.'" Like the whirlwind that he was, Turibius de Mogrovejo founded churches, new parishes in the Andes, religious houses, hospitals, and orphanages; and he established the first seminary in the New World. Turibius de Mogrovejo was also known to have had a great sense of humor. He faced his problems with absolute fearlessness, learned most of the native Indian dialects so that he could preach to people in their own language; and once, when he heard that some poor Indians were lost in the high Andes, he went in search of them himself until he found them. When he died on a journey into the Andes at the age of 66, he was the living embodiment of what it meant to be a priest in the most difficult and dangerous of circumstances. He had no precedents and so had to create his own.

The measure of a priest's confidence in God is the measure of his ability to face the new and totally unfamiliar—God's voice in a new language. He can listen to that voice and know freedom within that listening if, and only if, he has cultivated an interior life. Communion with the Trinity gives a priest the freedom to be obedient, creative, happy, and filled with pastoral charity. In prayer, a priest must enter into Christ's own pastoral charity; and then, mediocrity will never define his priesthood. May the life of prayer be the fount for the pastoral life of all priests. No contradiction to effective pastoral presence exists in deep contemplative prayer. The people do not want busy priests; they are thirsting for holy priests, priests that live in their presence as a burning reminder that God *is* all *in* all. Pope Benedict XVI said in his "Address to Clergy" in Freising, Germany in 2006:

> Therefore the time spent in direct encounter with God in prayer can rightly be described as the pastoral priority par excellence: It is the soul's breath, without which the priest necessarily remains breathless, deprived of the oxygen of optimism and joy, which he needs if he is to allow himself to be sent, day by day, as worker into the Lord's Harvest.

# Notes

1    *Upholding Mystery An Anthology of Contemporary Christian Poetry* David Impastato, ed. (New York: Oxford University Press, 1996), 16.

# Works Cited

Bernanos, George. *The Diary of a Country Priest* (New York: Carroll and Graf Publishers, Inc., 2001).

*Butler's Lives of the Saints.* Herbert J. Thurston, S.J. and Donald Attwater, eds. (New York: P. J. Kenedy and Sons, 1962).

Cather, Willa. *Death Comes for the Archbishop* (New York: Vintage Classics, Random House, 1990).

Green, Arthur. "Teachings of the Hasidic Masters," *Back to the Sources: Reading the Classic Jewish Texts.* ed. Barry W. Holtz (New York: Touchstone, 1984).

O'Connor, Edwin. *The Edge of Sadness* (Boston: Little Brown & Company, 1961).

LaVergne, TN USA
16 April 2010
179502LV00001B/2/P